# SOMETIMES I REALLY HATE YOU!

D0557287

# SOMETIMES I REALLY HATE YOU!

## DEWEY BERTOLINI

VICTOR BOOKS®

A DIVISION OF SCRIPTURE PRESS PUBLICATIONS INC.
USA CANADA ENGLAND

Scripture quotations, unless otherwise indicated, are from the *Holy Bible, New International Version*, © 1973, 1978, 1984, International Bible Society. Used by permission of Zondervan Bible Publishers. Scripture quotations marked NASB are from the *New American Standard Bible*, © the Lockman Foundation, 1960, 1962, 1963, 1968, 1971, 1972, 1973, 1975, 1977. Verses marked TLB are taken from *The Living Bible*, © 1971, Tyndale House Publishers, Wheaton, IL 60189. Used by permission.

### Library of Congress Cataloging-in-Publication Data

Bertolini, Dewey M.
    Sometimes I really hate you! / by Dewey M. Bertolini.
      p. cm. — Straight Talk series. 1)
    Summary: Discusses the bad effects that bitterness can cause and how Christians should deal with this negative emotion.
    ISBN 0-89693-041-6
    1. Revenge—Juvenile literature. 2. Hate—Juvenile literature. 3. Forgiveness—Religious aspects—Christianity—Juvenile literature. 4. Reconciliation—Religious aspects—Christianity—Juvenile literature. 5. Conversion—Juvenile literature. 6. Bertolini, Dewey M.—Juvenile literature. [1. Revenge. 2. Hate. 3. Forgiveness. 4. Conduct of life. 5. Christian life.]
    I. Title. II. Series.
    BV4627.R4B37 1991
    241'.3—dc20
                                       91-13923
                                           CIP
                                          AC

1 2 3 4 5 6 7 8 9 10 Printing/Year 95 94 93 92 91

# Contents

to

Dr. John R. Dunkin,
President Emeritus,
The Master's College.


God used this man
in my life to:


Lay my theological foundation;
Influence the formation of my
biblical convictions;
Serve as the man I emulated
during the crucial years
of my transition from
adolescence to adulthood.


To this model of faithful consistency
and selfless humility,
I gratefully and affectionately
dedicate this book.

# ACKNOWLEDGMENTS

My heartfelt thanks to . . .

Bob Phillips for the countless hours he has sacrificially devoted to me as my mentor in the field of publishing;

Bob Hilts for providing me with the platform from which the message of this book was prepared and proclaimed;

"Doc" Saunders for his invaluable insights;

Jane Vogel, world-class editor and mother *par excellence,* for transforming my dream into reality;

Tom Halstead for allowing me the time away from my office that I needed in bringing this project to completion;

My students at The Master's College, whom I love more than I can express for tolerating my absence during the writing of this book;

My dear wife, Rebecca, and two incredible children, David and Ashley, the treasures of my life, for cheering me on throughout the entire writing process;

My mother and sisters for allowing me to share with the world some of the more sensitive family memories we hold in common.

# PROLOGUE

*You will know the truth, and the truth will set you free.*
*(John 8:32)*

*J*esus, go to hell!" A more blatant blasphemy has never been uttered. Yet with all of the venom of a viper, Julie lashed out with these words.

When I first met her, she looked innocent enough—a typical high school student, certainly not a stand-out by any stretch of the imagination. Her friends had invited her to Hume Lake Christian Camp for a week in July and she had agreed to go. "Anything to get out of the house," she said later. During the recreation times she participated in the games, if only reluctantly. Most of the girls in Julie's cabin simply assumed that she needed more time to adjust to a new environment. Quickly I learned that this was not the case.

One night Julie approached me, obviously troubled

by something I had said in chapel. I opened the meeting by asking the 600 students present a probing question: "How many of you have been deeply hurt or offended by someone?" Nearly every hand went up. Julie sat in the back. She did not raise her hand, nor did she raise her eyes. She didn't look at me or in any way acknowledge my presence in the room.

Halfway through my message, she sprang from her seat and stormed out of the auditorium. Her counselor bolted out the door after her and found her sprawled out on the ground, sobbing uncontrollably.

"I hate him. I hate him so much. If only I could kill him. I hate him for what he did to me." Julie's counselor took the onslaught of the rampage. "I just want to hurt him. I just want to kill him!" Her screams for revenge shattered the otherwise tranquil sounds of the mountaintop at sunset.

Finally Julie agreed to talk to me. As long as I live, I will never forget the encounter that ensued. It seems like yesterday.

"Three months ago I was released from the hospital. You talk about hell? I've been there. They strapped me down to my bed, because they were afraid I'd try to kill myself again. And they were right. Look at my wrists—these scars are all I have to show for my efforts. I'm so screwed up. I can't even kill myself right!

"Why did my mother have to find me anyway?" she continued. "Why couldn't she just let me die? She doesn't want me around. My mom screamed at me all the way to the hospital. 'To hell with you, Julie. All you've ever done is ruin my life. You weren't even supposed to be born—you were a mistake! Did you hear me, Julie? A mistake. And after all

I've done for you, you go and pull a stupid thing like this. Maybe I should have just left you laying in your own blood.' "

More of the story unraveled as I sat quietly and listened.

"When I was five my dad started raping me. Do you have any idea what that's like? Laying in bed at night, scared to death that he's going to sneak in? Seeing that smirk on his face whenever my mom left to go shopping? The constant threats that he would take a knife and scar up my face if I ever told anyone? And I remember my friends telling me how lucky I was to have such a 'cool' dad. Try spending your whole life feeling like a damn piece of meat."

Julie looked hopeful momentarily.

"I just couldn't hold it in anymore so I told my friend, Sarah. She spread it all over the school. Now, they call me 'whore' and 'slut.' They don't know what it's like. They don't understand how badly it hurts.

"My parents hate my guts. They argue all the time—about money mostly. 'You're just in the way.' They tell me that over and over again. I'm just another mouth to feed. So I ran away.

"I got involved in drugs. I figured anything was better than remembering all the time. I've heard all the slogans: 'Don't do drugs, man. Just say no.' I decided maybe dying wasn't so bad. Tell me what I have to live for anyway?"

Julie's face suddenly froze with anger. "All I want is my dad dead. That's it. Other than that, I just want to be left alone. I don't want to hassle anyone and I don't want anyone to hassle me. There's nothing wrong with that.

"So I do a little crack. What's so bad about that?

The way I figured, my choice was a life of pain all the time or a little rush once in a while. Out on the street I'd do anything for a hit. I'd do sex for coke if I could get it. So I got it."

After an hour-and-a-half monologue, Julie finally began to wind down. I didn't know what to do or say. I had no way of verifying her story—she could have been lying for all I knew. One thing was for certain—there was no questioning her anger.

My words sounded empty when I asked if I could pray with her. "Me, pray? Yeah, right," she mocked.

I stumbled with my words. "It's really very simple, Julie. You can talk to God the same way you're talking to me. Tell Him anything you want."

"Anything?"

"Anything. Just pretend He's sitting right here next to you and tell Him what you would like Him to do for you."

Julie bowed her head and screamed: "Jesus, go to hell." Her words were piercing. Then she broke down and cried.

Trying my best to restore order to a bizarre situation, I asked, "Julie, why did you tell Him that?" She looked up wildly and shouted, "Because He killed my two best friends—Bill hanged himself in his closet using his own belt and Nancy shot herself in the head with her father's gun. God could have stopped them, but He didn't. He just let them die. He knew how badly that would hurt me. He's taken everything else away and now He's taken them. And I hate Him for it. I will always hate Him for it."

Bitterness—the hotbed issue of this decade. I have talked to literally thousands of young people and adults caught in the quicksand of their own fatal fantasies for revenge, motivated by a hidden hatred that burns in their systems like an acid. Often the root cause of a constellation of conflicts ranging from depression to suicide, anorexia to murder, no other single subject rears its ugly head with the same frequency or intensity as the topic of bitterness.

Whenever I address this subject in a public forum, hurting people come out of the woodwork—one after another, relating story after heartbreaking story, a veritable avalanche of emotions that has held innumerable individuals captive for months, years, or even decades. The Julies in our world cannot be counted.

And I understand. For nearly half my life, bitterness held me in its iron-fisted clasp. From the age of 7 to 24, one deadly deficiency destroyed me by degrees. For 17 years I allowed myself to hate a man. And that hatred nearly killed me.

*Sometimes I Really Hate You* is my story. Tragically, I have discovered that this tale can be retold repeatedly. I suspect that in many ways *Sometimes I Really Hate You* may be your story too. And while our details may differ, we hold the same pain and devastation in common.

I have not sought to research the subject from a technical point of view. And I have no desire to write as a theorist. Regurgitating another person's information will help no one. I write as one who has gone through it, feeling what you feel and experiencing what you experience. In a word, I write as one who understands.

I also write as one who has thoroughly studied the subject of bitterness from a biblical perspective. Having applied the results of my investigation to my own life, I offer myself to you as living proof that the Word of God can indeed set people free (John 8:32).

Something happened to me on that evening at Hume Lake, and I've not been able to rest since. I still remember Julie's eyes. I am haunted by her cries. I agonize over her pain, and the pain of countless others who have entrusted me with their stories. This book is their book, written in the hope that I can place in their hands something of lasting help and encouragement. I hope this book is your book as well, written with the prayer that you will find within its pages the answers to the questions that motivated you to pick it up. May God grant you a lasting victory as you seek to bring your own battle over bitterness to a triumphant conclusion.

# 1. THE LEGACY OF A LOSER

*Brothers, think of what you were when you were called. Not many of you were wise by human standards; not many were influential; not many were of noble birth. But God chose the foolish things of the world to shame the wise; God chose the weak things of the world to shame the strong. He chose the lowly things of this world and the despised things — and the things that are not — to nullify the things that are, so that no one may boast before him. (1 Corinthians 1:26-29)*

At seven years of age I began my battle over bitterness. Thirty-one years have come and gone, but my memories of a painful childhood linger to this day.

If you had stopped me on the street corner back then and asked me, "What's the one thing in life that you want?" I would have answered you without a moment's hesitation. I knew exactly what I wanted.

I don't think I would have answered in the same way as most kids my age because my desires did not focus on fire engines or radio-controlled cars. I lived with only one basic fantasy: I desperately wanted to know that my father loved me and was proud of me.

I'm sure you've seen proud fathers before—smiles on their faces, twinkles in their eyes, chest extended. And I'm sure you've heard the proclamations to anyone who will listen: "This is my son." I longed to hear those words—words that never came.

### Baby Blues

My father had never felt so exhilarated as the night of July 21, 1952. The nurse walked into the maternity waiting room at 7:35 P.M. and declared, "Mr. Bertolini, you have a bouncing baby boy!" Immediately Dad ran through the corridors of the hospital, shouting to everyone within the sound of his booming voice, "It's a boy, it's a boy!" He flung cigars everywhere.

Wouldn't you be excited to know your father was so elated at your birth? I was to discover one day, however, the reason behind his excitement. My father wanted a son who would grow up to be a professional athlete. From the time my small mind could begin to comprehend the English language my dad drilled me with the thought that I would someday win an Olympic gold medal, play in the Super Bowl, or become the starting shortstop in the All Star Game. There was no doubt in his mind that along the way I would sign a million-dollar contract and propel myself to national prominence!

I was a healthy baby boy—so everyone thought. My life proceeded without incident until I reached the age of 18 months. At that point it became clear that I could not fulfill my father's grandiose dreams due to a certain gland in my body which ceased to function properly. As a result I literally stopped growing!

Throughout junior high school, I was the shortest and least coordinated kid in the class. My father let everyone understand in no uncertain terms that he was ashamed of me. His rejection ignited a fire within me—a fire of hatred.

### Growin' Up Is Hard to Do

Several years ago, while playing the "Ungame," I landed on the space that read, "Tell It Like It Is." The corresponding card instructed me, "Describe the saddest day of your life." Two situations instantly popped into my mind, the first of which took place when I was seven.

Upon coming home from work one day, Dad excitedly called me into the living room and presented me with a paper bag. Inside it I discovered a full-size, official league football uniform—complete with pads, jersey, and a regulation football. The uniform fit me like a tent and my fingers couldn't grip the seams of the football. For 45 minutes my dad tried in vain to teach me how to throw a pass. Rather than form a spiral, again and again my throws tumbled end over end.

In a fit of rage, he ripped the ball out of my hand. I stood, paralyzed and shocked as I watched him move from door to door in the neighborhood, calling all of my friends together for a pick-up football scrimmage in the street. When the teams were organized and ready to play, I asked, "Where do you want me to play, Dad?" He whirled around and shouted at me at the top of his voice, "Sit down and shut up! No son of mine is going to embarrass me in public!"

My friends said nothing—nor did I. With every ounce of strength within me, I tried in vain to hold back a torrent of tears. On that overcast afternoon, a part of me died. The fire of bitterness within me began to grow even larger.

The second "Tell It Like It Is" event took place on a sunny Sunday afternoon at McCambridge Baseball Park in Burbank, California. Again, the occasion revolved around my father's frustration with my inability to play sports. The memory of that moment haunts me to this day.

Dad sat me down on the bleachers, the third base side of diamond #1, five benches from the top. For two hours he yelled at me: "Why can't you play like the other kids play? Why can't you catch like they catch, throw like they throw, hit like they hit?" And then he said something that I will never forget: "Dewey, I wonder sometimes if you will ever grow up to be a man." His words still cut like a knife. I felt as if someone had plunged a dagger into my gut and twisted it. Two emotions surged through my system: a hatred for my father beyond description and a burning passion to prove my father wrong.

Do you have any idea how badly it hurts to wake up every morning and look into the mirror only to see the reflection of a loser? Have you ever been forced to brush the teeth and comb the hair of a failure? I carried that pain every day of my life because, according to my dad's definition, that's exactly what I was. The fire inside me continued to flame.

In the years that followed, my bitterness continued to grow, spurred on by my father's unreasonable expectations not only of me, but also of my mother and two younger sisters. I vividly remember his returning home one night drunk. My mom drove my sisters and me to a motel where we spent the night. We literally feared for our very lives.

Other times I watched in horror as my dad took a knife and shredded my mother's dresses. I heard my dad threaten my mom with bodily injury on countless occasions. The winds of his assaults continued to fan the flames of my hatred.

### Bad News/Good News
When I reached the age of 16, my life took an unexpected twist. I will never forget that fateful evening. I knew something strange was about to happen—my parents were not fighting as they normally did. Mom finally called me into their bedroom, sat me down on the bed, looked straight at me and said, "I have some very bad news for you. Your father and I have decided to get a divorce." I sat still for a moment, fully expecting her to say more, thinking to myself, "So what's the bad news?" I wanted to throw a party on the spot!

I was enough of an actor to play the part of a bereaved child. As I carried his bags out to the car, I turned to my dad and said sympathetically, "Dad, I sure hate to see you go. Thanks for the memories. Keep in touch."

As I watched the taillights fade and finally disappear, I made a vow. I promised myself that I would never see nor speak to that man again. I wanted nothing to do with him under any circumstances. I

kept my promise. Whenever he called, I hung up.
Every card and letter suffered a certain demise: I
ripped, cut, and mutilated each one to my heart's
delight. He got the message fast: "Dad, you will find
absolutely no room in my life for you." And the fire
raged on!

I used to pray back then, "God, I don't know where
my father is right now, but You do. I can't see what
he's doing, but you can. I've heard that You've got
some lightning bolts up there in heaven—some big
ones (the 220 volt variety). And I've heard that
You're a pretty good shot. I wish You'd unleash one
of them now and blow him away." My fantasies ran
wild. I laid awake at night planning and plotting my
father's execution. I wanted nothing more than to see
him suffer. The fire now burned out of control.

## Turning Point
Several months after my parents' divorce, I invited
Jesus Christ into my life. I had never heard a sermon
before. I did not know a single verse of biblical truth.
But on an otherwise uneventful evening in July 1969,
my life underwent a radical transformation.

Bored mindless, I turned on the television in my
bedroom that night and began flipping through the
channels. Suddenly these words captured my attention: "God chose the weak things of the world. He
chose the lowly things of this world and the despised
things. He loves losers. He loves failures. He loves
nobodies. He loves rejects. He loves you just the way
you are. Others may have rejected you, made fun of
you, put you down, ridiculed you, but Jesus Christ
never will. He died for you, shed His blood for you,
and rose from the dead for you." Billy Graham's

words riveted me to the set. I had never heard such statements before. I sat transfixed throughout the entire telecast.

Dr. Graham was holding his crusade at the Madison Square Garden in New York as I watched from my bedroom in California. When he gave the invitation to receive Christ, a multitude of people began to pour onto the arena floor. I remember saying to myself, "I would give anything to be there right now so that I could receive Christ, too!" At that precise moment, Dr. Graham looked into the television camera and said, "You who are watching this telecast can make the same commitment these people are making here tonight." I knelt by my bed and prayed a very simple but extremely sincere prayer: "Jesus, I feel like a loser. I didn't think anybody loved losers. I didn't think anybody loved me. I don't have anything to offer You. All I can say is, if You are willing to take me like I am, I give myself to You." My bedroom suddenly became my gateway "into the kingdom of the Son He loves" (Colossians 1:13).

I know the stock testimony should go something like this: "I got off my knees and I felt an overflowing love for my father throughout my body. I called him on the phone, we kissed, made up, and now live happily together." Not so with me.

Nevertheless, I began to read my Bible. In three months I completed the entire New Testament. During that time I came upon startling statements such as, "Husbands, love your wives just as Christ loved the church and gave Himself up for her" (Ephesians 5:25). I thought to myself, "Right! My dad loved my mom so much that he pulled out a switchblade and shredded her clothes."

Another one read, "Fathers, do not exasperate your children; instead, bring them up in the training and instruction of the Lord" (Ephesians 6:4). "What a joke!" I said to myself. "You tell him, God. Tell him how he shouldn't assassinate me in front of all my friends. Tell him how he shouldn't humiliate me with his endless verbal assaults." My reading only confirmed for me how greatly my father had failed as a dad. The fire exploded into a towering inferno.

The root of bitterness is probably the most destructive of all human emotions. The scars can last a lifetime. One last example graphically illustrates the point:

During my senior year in high school, things started to change. I began to grow physically — not a lot — but any growth came as a welcome surprise! Along with my increased stature I also became better coordinated.

Some of my friends formed a city league softball team and invited me to try out. With fear and trepidation I arrived at the park, glove in hand and my ego on the line. I had never survived a cut before. Why should things be any different now?

The coach yelled, "Hey, Dewey, take third." He shot some balls down the line. To the amazement of my friends, I caught every one of them! Each of my throws hit the first baseman at his belt buckle. I ended up playing every inning of every game.

It was a Cinderella season. Only one other team besides ours went undefeated. The showdown came on the last day of league competition. Before the game, the officials rolled out a table of trophies. As they glistened in the sunlight, I began to salivate — I wanted one so badly.

The game was a spectator's dream. We battled for six innings, playing to a 6–6 tie. The opposing team scored one run in the top of the seventh and we moved into the bottom of the last trailing 7–6.

Our first batter hit a sharp ground ball to short. He flew down the line and stretched for the first base bag, but the throw beat him by a split second. One out. The next batter hit a flare into right-center field that dropped for a base hit. One on; one out. The third batter hit a fly ball to center. One on; two outs. I grabbed my bat and slowly walked up to the plate.

I fell into a trance. With the tying run on first, we needed a home run to win. I had never hit a home run in my life. I planted my right foot and settled in.

Honestly, I did not see the first pitch. I mean, this guy was throwing smoke. How in the world do you hit a sound? I heard only the "whoosh" it made as it flew past and the smack of the ball as it hit the catcher's glove. "Strike one!" shouted the umpire.

I could feel the perspiration beading up on my forehead and felt the intense pressure of the entire season weighing upon me. I swung my bat back and forth and squinted as I tried desperately to focus my eyes. I watched the pitcher begin his wind-up. Whoosh. "Strike two!" yelled the umpire.

Every guy on the team was pacing in the dugout, shouting encouragements and direction. People were waving, chanting and cheering from every direction. The entire season—the championship—the whole world, so it seemed, rested on my shoulders. The trophies taunted me with their diamond-like reflections.

I honestly don't remember what happened next. After hearing the smack of the bat on the ball, I instinctively started running to first base. The ball flew into left-center field and rolled all the way to the wall. I ran like the seat of my pants was on fire. As I rounded second, I saw the third base coach waving the runner home. I knew we had at least tied the game! But we needed one more run. Then I saw the coach waving me home! As I approached the plate, everyone in the dugout screamed, "Slide, slide!" I went into a three-point, 747 landing, hit the ground, and somehow rolled over onto my back. Everything seemed to happen in slow motion. As I moved toward the plate I could see the ball sail over my head. The catcher applied a perfect tag, dust flew everywhere, and a deathly silence fell over the crowd. All eyes were riveted on the umpire. At that moment he held the destinies of two teams in the palm of his hand. After what seemed like an eternity, he finally shouted, "Safe!" The crowd went wild.

Now, ball players sometimes do weird things when they win. You should have seen the guys on my team. High-fives, hugs, and cheers filled the air. A party was in full swing all over the dugout. We felt like we had just won the World Series!

No one noticed when I quietly left the commotion in the dugout and walked up the third base line. No one seemed to catch my glassy-eyed gaze as I straddled the third base bag. And nobody paid any attention to me when I stood, staring at the bleachers.

Do you have any idea where I hit that championship-clinching home run? God has a way of remembering details. I hit that home run on a piece of real estate known as McCambridge Park, diamond #1. My dad wasn't there, but in my mind's eye I saw him—five benches down from the top. I had waited six years for that moment. With tears streaming down my face I whispered angrily, "Dad, that one was for you. Are you happy now?"

To this day, I cannot walk onto a softball field, or put a glove on my hand, or pick up a bat without hearing a faint echo in my mind asking, "Why can't you hit like they hit? Why can't you catch like they catch? Why can't you play like they play?"

I have not shared my story with you because I wanted to generate a pity party for myself. I wrote my story because I wanted you to know where I'm coming from. I've tried to write honestly. For many years, I continued to refuse to allow my father to speak to me or see me. But while I separated myself from my father physically, I could not separate myself from him emotionally. The blaze of hatred within me seemed never to die.

Suddenly, unexpectedly, the separation came to a screeching halt. Out of nowhere, my father came crashing into my life. The trauma of that moment shakes me to this day. A cabin in the woods was the place where a chance encounter became for me a crossroad.

When I saw my dad, I wanted to grab something, anything, and hurl it at him full force. My dad reached out his hand to shake mine. I trembled uncontrollably with rage. I clenched my fists às Dad took a step in my direction. What I did in the next 30 seconds forever changed the rest of my life. You'll read about it in a later chapter.

## In the Trenches:
## Waging Your Own War from Within

1. Now that you know my story, can you relate to any of my experiences? Did you sense any similarities to your own situation, in terms of your feelings, reactions, thoughts or actions?

2. Is there anyone in your life you have wanted to hurt or destroy? Have you allowed your own fantasies of revenge to run wild? Did you ever ask God to unload one of His lightning bolts at anyone? Do you continue to feel that way now?

3. I would not be qualified to address this issue with you if I had not first worked through "the battle over bitterness" in my own life. We'll get to the details later. But for now, I simply want to state that a complete healing is possible. If God can change my heart, He can certainly change yours. If you want to know how, please keep reading. If your attitude dictates a refusal to change "no matter what," then definitely keep reading. I wrote the next chapter especially for you.

# 2. SLOW BUT CERTAIN SUICIDE

*See to it that no one misses the grace of God and that no bitter root grows up to cause trouble and defile many. (Hebrews 12:15)*

"I hate my dad!" shouted one teen. "No one in my family gives a damn whether I live or die," screamed another. These kinds of devastating declarations have assaulted my senses for years.

A high school girl, while sobbing uncontrollably, clung to me as if for dear life. What could I say as she related to me the fact that her 22-year-old brother earned his living by dealing drugs? "He pinned me down on the floor and tried to force me to swallow one of his pills. He said to me, 'If I can get you hooked, you'll have to buy your supply from me.'

Why does my brother hate me so much?"

A junior high boy crumbled emotionally as he shared his story. "All my friends call me ugly. 'Hi, Ugly. How are you doing, Ugly?' " Over the years, I have learned that in certain situations I possess the potential of creating or destroying a very fragile life. This situation was no different. With a pleading look in his eyes, he asked me what may well rank as the most important question he will ever ask anyone. "Do you think I'm ugly?" I threw my arms around him and yelled, "No way!" On an obscure little sidewalk in front of a nondescript little house the two of us spontaneously broke into tears.

Welcome to a day in the life of Dewey Bertolini. In my 19 years of working with troubled teenagers, I have experienced practically nothing more excruciating than having to hear innumerable sordid scandals and scenarios in the lives of young people.

Do you know what hurts me even more? Watching the slow but steady self-destruction that results when someone allows an attitude of bitterness—like a malignant tumor—to take root, fester, spread, and ultimately destroy (Hebrews 12:15). I have discovered in my life through personal experience and through the observation of others that bitterness, when it takes root, is nothing less than slow but certain suicide.

### Bitterness—It's More Than Skin Deep
In light of this, allow me to isolate two important words.

(1) **Root:** not a glamorous word by anybody's standard, but used in this context, "root" serves as a helpful metaphor.

Every spring, with spade in hand, my dad and I

stepped out onto the lawn, ready to reclaim the precious turf we had lost to the weeds. He would always remind me, "Whenever you pull out a weed, be sure you take it up by its roots."

In the process I discovered five fascinating facts about these unsightly "subterranean plant parts":

● Roots grow invisibly, below the surface of the soil. *The Sunset Western Garden Book*[1] states "At the root ends are tender root tips. Each contains a growing point that continually produces elongating cells. These cells push the roots deeper and farther out into the moist soil." A root of bitterness grows imperceptibly yet steadily millimeter by millimeter. Mine did. So does yours.

● Roots sap the soil of chemical substances. "The first single root soon begins to send out tiny white rootlets, which draw in the chemical substances needed for growth." Bitterness can sap your system of much needed energy, leaving you vanquished, bankrupting you physically, mentally, emotionally, and spiritually.

● Roots give birth to new weeds. If left unchecked, this spreading process will take over and eventually destroy the most manicured lawns.

● Roots can harden as they develop a "skin-like covering similar to bark." The longer you allow your bitterness to spread its tenacious tentacles throughout your heart, the harder your heart will become.

● "The entire root system anchors the plant in the soil." The writer of Hebrews wrote this warning to his readers: "Throw off everything that hinders and the sin that so easily entangles, and let us run with perseverance the race marked out for us" (Hebrews 12:1). The Christian life has been compared to a race.

Some people cruise along in high gear. Others hit the skids and spend their lives spinning their wheels.

What kinds of entangling sins will force you into the pits for repairs? Fourteen verses later the writer concisely considers the most entangling sin of all: "See to it that . . . no bitter root grows up." Bitterness will not only slow you down in the race, it will anchor you to the track!

The potential consequences of bitterness can be damaging indeed. But they can also become deadly. Consider the second word:

(2) **Suicide:** In this context, this overused word provides the most descriptive designation possible. Defined simply as "the intentional taking of one's own life," suicide certainly summarizes the long-range consequences of bitterness.

Suicide does not have to take place in one isolated and immediate act. Suicide can take place over many months or, in some cases, years. Any willful act of self-destruction comes under the broad umbrella of "suicide." Bitterness tragically qualifies as both "willful" and "self-destructive." Bitterness is indeed nothing less than slow but certain suicide. "The torture of our anger eats us alive. The carcass we eat at the banquet table of anger is ours."[2] To my surprise and disgust I discovered that my own bitterness was eating me alive. My research revealed that bitterness possesses the potential of destroying you and me in six deadly ways:

## Physical Destruction
When God put you and me together, He did not create us with the capacity to harbor hatred. When Jesus told Peter to forgive his brother "seventy times sev-

en" (Matthew 18:22, marginal reference) He didn't merely utter a pious platitude aimed at bringing good cheer to a war-torn world. Jesus handed Peter one of the most important principles relative to maintaining sound physical health.

Bitterness acts as a poison in our systems. Under the heading, "The High Cost of Getting Even," Dr. S.I. McMillen persuasively points out that bitterness can in time result in "ulcerative colitis, toxic goiters, high blood pressure and scores of other diseases" including heart disease, strokes, arteriosclerosis, kidney disease, headaches, and ulcers of the stomach and intestine.[3] Other physical symptoms can include insomnia, fatigue, or loss of appetite.

Bitterness can also result in so-called psychosomatic illnesses. "Headaches or bodily aches and pains that seem to have no basis in organic pathology often cover up emotional conflicts."[4]

## Mental Destruction
Dr. McMillen writes,

> The moment I start hating a man, I become his slave. I can't enjoy my work any more because he even controls my thoughts. My resentments produce too many stress hormones in my body and I become fatigued after only a few hours of work. The work I formerly enjoyed is now drudgery. Even vacations cease to give me pleasure. It may be a luxurious car that I drive along a lake fringed with the autumnal beauty of maple, oak and birch. As far as my experience of pleasure is concerned, I might as well be driving a wagon in mud and rain.

The man I hate hounds me wherever I go. I can't escape his tyrannical grasp on my mind. When the waiter serves me porterhouse steak with French fries, asparagus, crisp salad, and strawberry shortcake smothered with ice cream, it might as well be stale bread and water. My teeth chew the food and I swallow it, but the man I hate will not permit me to enjoy it.

The man I hate may be many miles from my bedroom; but more cruel than any slave driver, he whips my thoughts into such a frenzy that my innerspring mattress becomes a rack of torture. The lowliest of the serfs can sleep, but not I. I really must acknowledge the fact that I am a slave to every man on whom I pour the vials of my wrath.[5]

Can you identify with Dr. McMillen's confession? Solomon certainly could. He captured the same thought when he lamented, "Better a meal of vegetables where there is love than a fattened calf with hatred" (Proverbs 15:17). Solomon apparently experienced firsthand the mental anguish that can result when someone's brain becomes entangled in a relentless web as the roots of bitterness spread throughout the mind.

### Emotional Destruction
The connection between ongoing hatred and the lack of emotional health cannot be ignored. Just as prolonged exercise drains our bodies of physical energy, so bitterness drains our systems of much needed emotional energy. The results can be overwhelming.

Paul commanded, "Do not let the sun go down while you are still angry" (Ephesians 4:26). Dr. Meier points out one practical reason behind the imperative. "Pent-up anger is the root of nearly all clinical depression."[6]

One girl described her depression as "sinking into a bottomless pit and there's nothing I can do to stop it." She tried desperately to act and feel "happy," but simply could not muster up enough emotional energy to pull it off. Her friends and even her youth pastor berated her for not displaying the "joy of the Lord," branding her a sinner and plunging her even deeper into that "bottomless pit."

Bitterness-induced depression can lead to a variety of harmful behavior patterns. "Depression feeds on itself as one's thinking becomes progressively more painful. People who feel hopeless, helpless, worthless, and guilty become very self-critical and debasing. Cyclical in effect, inappropriate thinking results in irresponsible behavior, which increases depression, which in turn stimulates more inappropriate thinking."[7] Meier further states, "When adults become depressed, they look and act depressed; when adolescents become depressed, however, they usually act out their depression. In place of a sad affect, an adolescent may appear belligerent, sarcastic, or hostile. Gripped by emotional depression, an otherwise moral teenager may begin to steal, lie, use drugs, or act out sexually."[8]

He may even attempt to take his own life. The "slow but certain suicide" of bitterness may tragically result in a sudden and catastrophic end to the feelings of anger, depression, and hopelessness that bitterness often brings.

## Spiritual Destruction

Bitterness often dramatically affects a person's relationship with God. We humans are notorious for blaming God for our problems. The thinking often goes something like this: "I didn't choose to be born. I certainly didn't choose this family! God is obviously powerful enough to prevent these situations if He wants to. Why did God let this happen to me anyway?"

I will never forget the first time I came face-to-face with the rage this kind of rationale can produce. A girl in my college group was savagely raped. The first time she saw me after the attack she blurted out the question, "If God is so loving and if He is so powerful, then why did He allow me to be raped?"

After his best friend died in a fireball collision involving a drunk driver, a student asked me, "Why did God kill Steve? Why didn't He make the car veer to the left instead of to the right?" His anger quickly floated from the drunk driver who caused the accident to God who allowed it.

A linebacker, after being carried off the field with a shattered knee, screamed to me, "All I ever wanted to do was play football. Now it's over. Why didn't God stop him from hitting me?"

The object of our bitterness can shift at a moment's notice. We sometimes think of God as a magical genie who exists to grant us our every whim and wish. When He doesn't deliver the way we think He should, we can strike out at Him in anger quickly. The results of these kinds of responses can be spiritually paralyzing.

As a youth speaker, the greatest challenge I face is the need to guide biblical truth around a student's mental roadblocks. When I invite teenagers to commit their lives to Christ, I know that some are thinking, "Yeah, right, trust Him with my eternity? I can't even trust Him with my family!" The simple word "Father" has become a loaded term. Many young people project upon God, their heavenly Father, the same warped characteristics their abusive earthly fathers possess. "Worship a God like that? No way!"

Specifically, what kinds of conflicts can bitterness cause in a person's spiritual life? If you have ever asked one or more of the following questions, be encouraged! You are in good company. Even the godly men who wrote the Psalms struggled with the same doubts.

● "Does God really exist? I come to Him with all of these problems and nothing changes. In fact they sometimes get worse." David cried out in despair, "My God, my God, why have You forsaken me? Why do You refuse to help me or even to listen to my groans? Day and night I keep on weeping, crying for Your help, but there is no reply" (Psalm 22:1-2, TLB).

● "Am I really a Christian?" A young person often senses the hypocrisy of worshipping someone he has come to hate. David's plea sounds strangely similar, "Restore to me again the joy of Your salvation, and make me willing to obey You" (Psalm 51:12, TLB). The compilers of *The Life Application Bible* perfectly summarized the situation:

> Has sin driven a wedge between you and God, making Him seem distant? David felt this way. In his prayer to God he cried, "Restore to me again the joy of Your salvation." God wants us to be close to Him and to experience His full and

complete life. But sin that remains unconfessed makes such intimacy impossible. Confess your sin to God. You may still have to face the consequences, as David did, but God will give back the joy of your relationship with Him.[9]

● "Can I really trust God? He certainly has not proven Himself trustworthy in my situation." David faced the hopelessness of life apart from a trustworthy God when He declared, "If You refuse to answer me, I might as well give up and die" (Psalm 28:1, TLB).

● "Can God really forgive me? How can He forgive me when I cannot forgive Him or the people who so deeply hurt me? Has God turned His back on me?" Asaph asked the same questions in his own way. "I cry to the Lord; I call and call to Him. Oh, that he would listen. I am in deep trouble and I need His help so much. All night long I pray, lifting my hands to heaven, pleading. Has the Lord rejected me forever? Will He never again be favorable?" (Psalm 77:1-2, 7, TLB)

Jesus' warning comes to mind: "Your heavenly Father will forgive you if you forgive those who sin against you; but if you refuse to forgive them, He will not forgive you" (Matthew 6:14-15, TLB). Listen to the explanation given in *The Life Application Bible:*

Jesus gives a startling warning about forgiveness: if we refuse to forgive others, He will also refuse to forgive us. Why? Because when we don't forgive others, we are denying our common ground as sinners in need of God's forgiveness. God's forgiveness of sin is not the direct result of our forgiving others, but it is based on our realizing what forgiveness means (see Eph. 4:32). How forgiven would you be if God's forgiveness were based on the way you forgive others? It is easy to ask God for forgiveness, but difficult to grant it to others. Whenever we ask God to forgive us for sin, we should ask ourselves, "Have I forgiven the people who have hurt or wronged me?"[10]

● "Does God really love me? Can He possibly love someone who holds a grudge against Him?" Asaph questioned God's unconditional love when he asked, "Is His lovingkindness gone forever? Has He slammed the door in anger on His love? And I said: 'This is my fate, that the blessings of God have changed to hate' " (Psalm 77:8-9, TLB).

● "Can God really empower my life? How can God's Spirit fill someone who consciously resists Him?" He can't. In fact, when you and I allow hatred to continue, we bring heartache to the Holy Spirit. Paul wrote, "Do not grieve the Holy Spirit of God" (Ephesians 4:30). How do we grieve the Holy Spirit? By refusing to obey the command given in the next verses, "Get rid of all bitterness, rage and anger." "Be kind and compassionate to one another, forgiving each other, just as in Christ God forgave you."

David so insightfully illustrated this possibility when he pleaded with God, "Don't take your Holy Spirit from me" (Psalm 51:1). Would God ever take the Holy Spirit away from us? Yes, in this sense:

If God reveals harshness in you and you decide not to deal with it, you will grieve the

Spirit of God and you'll come short of the grace of God (Heb. 12:15-17). You actually settle for bitterness instead of the energy of the Holy Spirit. Understand, it's possible to harbor anger, retain it, and be filled with the Spirit, but it becomes impossible after God has revealed the condition to you—unless you are willing to deal with it. It's a principle: You cannot be aware of roots of bitterness and be filled with the Holy Spirit. The two are mutually incompatible.

"I'll trade you my bitterness for God's power in you." That's the devil's deal. But it's like selling Boardwalk to someone who owns Park Place. It's a bad trade. Bitterness eats you alive and leaves you battered and bruised.[11]

Have you been "battered and bruised" spiritually by your own root of bitterness? I have taken several paragraphs to illustrate the fact that bitterness can result in devastating spiritual consequences. Please, consider the damage that has and will result in your life and determine to take the appropriate steps necessary to pluck this weed up by its roots.

### Social Destruction
Bitter people tend to walk through life with chips on their shoulders. Do you know anyone who is negative all the time? Do you have any friends who have the uncanny ability of walking into a room and killing a party? Do any of your friends use profanity continuously? You can often pick them out of a crowd because of their negative attitudes and pugnacious spirits. They act as if they are mad at the world.

When I asked you the questions about your

friends, did you tragically think of yourself? Perhaps the greatest hindrance to your own friendships is your own bitterness. The writer to the Hebrews correctly referred to a root of bitterness springing up "to cause trouble and defile many" (Hebrews 12:15). Bitterness does not only affect the one who is bitter—it affects every relationship that person has.

### Personal Destruction

This point is the most frightening of all. Unfortunately, I had to learn it the hard way. Did you realize that if you harbor bitterness against someone, given enough time you will turn out just like that person?

I used to say to myself, "I will never grow up to be like my father. Never!" A few weeks before I got married, I received a sobering surprise about my life.

My mother loves my wife. She loved her like her own daughter even before we got married. She wasn't trying to be unkind or unloving. She merely wanted my fiancé to know what she was getting into. She took my wife-to-be out to lunch and shared the following with her. "Dewey's dad and I got a divorce several years ago. There were things about that man I couldn't stand to live with. I wanted you to know, before you marry my son, that Dewey is just like him."

Can you even begin to imagine how I felt when Becky shared that conversation with me? I immediately reacted in anger—which is just how my dad would have reacted. After some reflection, however, I had to admit that my mom hit the bull's-eye. I had become the very thing I vowed I would never become.

The following reference may help to explain my

point. Proverbs states, "As a man thinks within himself, so is he" (Proverbs 23:7, NASB). Proverbs 4:23 warns, "Above all else, guard your heart, for it is the wellspring of life." You have been told, "You are what you eat." Not so. You are what you think! We have already noted that when a person becomes bitter he tends to think often about the person he hates. When you are angry at someone, do you think about his good characteristics or about the things you despise the most?

For years I allowed my mind to grind away at the negative thoughts I had against my father. In time I began to translate every one of those thoughts into attitudes and actions. I became just like the one I hated the most.

You might be thinking, "That's it; I'm doomed. I'll never get married. I'll never have children. I'm destined to failure for the rest of my life." If so, I've got some great news for you. The negative impact of your bitterness can be reversed—if you respond correctly.

If you continue to maintain an attitude of resentment toward the one you hate, you will hurt a lot of people (especially those who are closest to you) in the process. But if you let go of your bitterness, God's power can transform even the hardest of hearts into a heart of love that will greatly benefit everyone who knows you.

### Watergate Remembered

Former President Richard Nixon will be remembered by historians in a number of ways. He distinguished himself as a great statesman and champion of peace. He opened doors of diplomacy that had been bolted shut for decades. But he also resigned the presidency while wallowing in the wastelands of the Watergate scandal.

On the eve of his untimely departure from the White House, Mr. Nixon met with his White House staff for the last time. His recollections of his five and one-half years in office were poignant; his challenges for the future, perceptive. When he stepped out from behind his podium, there wasn't a dry eye in the house. Of all the words he uttered while in office, none was perhaps more insightful than the remarks he made at the conclusion of this, his last speech.

To fully appreciate his final farewell you must understand the situation. As President, Mr. Nixon was the most powerful human being on the planet. He made some mistakes. He deserved his retribution. His demise, however, came about largely because of a few individuals who abandoned any sense of loyalty to the President. Mr. Nixon, I am sure, felt betrayed and belittled before the American citizenry. He had ample reasons to harbor bitterness. He did, after all, fall from the pinnacle of the Presidency into the pit of his own political purgatory. In light of this, consider his closing remarks: "Always remember, others may hate you, but those who hate you don't win unless you hate them—and then you destroy yourself."[12]

Yes, bitterness is nothing less than slow but certain suicide.

**In the Trenches:**
**Waging Your Own War from Within**

Did you find any surprises in this chapter? Did the
severity of the potential consequences frighten you?
Do you sense that you have already begun to experience some of the damage bitterness can cause? Allow
me to suggest the following:

1. Review the six categories of destruction listed in
this chapter. Which category causes you the most
concern? Take an inventory of your life. Have any of
these problems begun to manifest themselves?

2. Memorize Ephesians 4:29-32. Take out a sheet of
paper and answer the following questions:
    a. Do any unwholesome words come out of your
mouth? If so, how often and in what situations?
    b. Do you consciously look for opportunities in
which you can encourage other people, or do you
tend to degrade and ridicule people? Would malicious
gossip qualify as "unwholesome talk"?
    c. What does the phrase "Do not grieve the Holy
Spirit" mean? How does grieving the Holy Spirit relate to the topic of "bitterness"?
    d. How do the words "bitterness, rage and anger,
brawling and slander, along with every form of malice" relate to each other?
    e. According to verse 32, what constitutes the op-
posite of bitterness?
    f. What command is given in verse 32? How did
God forgive you?

3. Now that you have picked apart this most important passage, how does its truth relate to the consequences of bitterness and anger in your life?

# 3. FORGIVE AND FORGET? GIVE ME A BREAK!

*Then Peter came to Jesus and asked, "Lord, how many times shall I forgive my brother when he sins against me? Up to seven times?" Jesus answered, "I tell you, not seven times but seventy-seven times." (Matthew 18:21-22)*

Words. They continually bombard me. At times I feel as though I am swirling in a sea of synonyms.

Many words assault our senses every day. *Funk and Wagnalls* notes this interesting fact: "It has been estimated that the present English vocabulary consists of more than one million words, including slang and dialect expressions and scientific and technical terms, many of which only came into use after the middle of the twentieth century. *The English vocabu-*

*lary is more extensive than that of any other language in the world"* (emphasis mine).[1]

Of course some words are far more important than others. In fact, my life has been radically redirected because of the impact of just a handful of words.

In this chapter, I want to expose you to one of the most revolutionary words in my vocabulary. Apart from it I would have no relationship with Jesus Christ. And without it I would be consumed with an overwhelming attitude of resentment and hatred. Its importance cannot be surpassed by any other word in the English language.

Mentioned over 100 times in the Bible, this word provides us with the key to overcoming bitterness. Have you ventured a guess? The word is "forgive." You and I must learn how to forgive those people who deeply hurt and offend us.

### Me Forgive? You've Got to Be Kidding!

I wish that I could observe your facial expressions and reactions as you read this chapter. Although this is impossible, I can predict that you just responded to the concept of forgiveness in one of three possible ways:

(1) You blew it off as you thought to yourself, "Here we go again. I've heard it a thousand times before. Just what I need, some trite Christian cliché. It's not as simple as forgive and forget and live happily ever after." If you just reacted in this way, keep reading. You will discover a greater wealth of insight concerning forgiveness than you ever thought possible!

(2) You gripped the book a little tighter and began to read a little faster. You realized that you have

finally found the answer you've been searching for. You can't wait to see what's coming. If this describes your response, I can assure you that you will not be disappointed.

(3) You felt a twinge of anger. "What? Me forgive? You can't feel the pain I carry every day of my life. I'd rather die than forgive him!" May I remind you from the last chapter that if these words describe your response, you may well get your wish? The bitterness you carry can end up killing you.

Talk is cheap. Nothing would be easier for me than to sit at a typewriter and regurgitate a textbook definition of the word "forgive." However, I can assure you that my talk is not cheap. I stood at the crossroads of this life-and-death struggle. You stand there now. Your response to this issue will dramatically influence the rest of your life.

"Forgive" is a multifaceted word. Like a radiant diamond refracting a beam of light into a rainbow of colors, the word "forgive" summarizes a diversity of insights that can be viewed from a variety of vantage points. For this reason I want to examine several definitions of the word, and I encourage you to select the one that suits your situation best.

### Forgiveness Is Wiping the Slate Completely Clean (Ephesians 4:32)

Paul wrote, "Be kind and compassionate to one another, forgiving each other, just as in Christ God forgave you." How did God forgive us? He erased the chalk board completely and He holds our sins against us no longer.

When we received Jesus Christ, He immediately hurled "all our iniquities into the depths of the sea"

(Micah 7:19). David declared, "As far as the east is from the west, so far has He removed our transgressions from us" (Psalm 102:12).

Why did David use the phrase "east is from the west" rather than "north is from the south?" The distance between the north pole and south pole is finite and measurable. By way of contrast, no one can determine where east begins and west ends. There exists an infinite and immeasurable distance between the two! Do you understand the significance of this? God completely separated us from all of our sins. In the same way, God commands us to completely wipe the slate clean.

### Forgiveness Is Realizing That God Will Use Our Painful Circumstances to Accomplish His Purposes (Genesis 50:20)

Would you like to participate in a public opinion poll? Here's the question: Who in the Bible would you choose as the most likely candidate for developing a root of bitterness? I can think of several possibilities. Tamar became a victim of incest (Genesis 38). Naomi endured a famine, lost her home, husband, and two sons. She then changed her name to Mara, which means "bitter" (Ruth 1:20). But for this discussion we will focus on a young man by the name of Joseph (Genesis 39).

At the age of 17, Joseph watched in horror as his 10 brothers turned against him. Motivated by their own jealousy, they sold him as a slave. Then they lied to their father, Jacob, by telling him that a wild animal had gored him to death. They watched as a band of gypsies took Joseph hostage into a foreign country.

Separated from his family and friends by hundreds

of miles, with no possible means of escape, Joseph experienced years of agonizing loneliness. He resisted the waves of seduction that came rushing in upon him, spawned by the alluring advances of his master's wife. He was sentenced to prison, confined because of a trumped-up accusation. Jospeh endured separation from his family and homeland for over 13 years!

Consider for a moment that you are Jospeh. Who are your targets of bitterness? Your brothers for betraying you. Your father for favoring you, thus triggering this scenario of suffering. The woman for casting her lustful looks in your direction. Your master for believing a lie. Your God, who was certainly powerful enough to prevent any of this from ever taking place.

Through a series of dramatic events, Joseph lived to see the day of his release from prison, his promotion to the second most powerful position in all of Egypt, and his reunion with his brothers. He held the opportunity for revenge in the palm of his hand.

Joseph could have had his brothers arrested, but he didn't. He could have had them beaten, but he said No. He could have had them executed, but he resisted. They trembled in his presence.

This scene describes the backdrop for 33 of the most radical words ever uttered in human history. What would you say after 13 years of waiting and dreaming about this moment? "Joseph said to them, 'Don't be afraid. Am I in the place of God? You intended to harm me, but *God intended it for good* to accomplish what is now being done, the saving of many lives' " (Genesis 50:19-20, emphasis mine).

In the midst of a seemingly hopeless situation, Joseph had no idea that God was controlling the evil intentions of men for His own purposes. Joseph saved entire nations from the grip of a seven-year famine. It would not be overstating the case to say that you and I would not be here today if Joseph had not first been sold as a slave. What man intends for evil, God will always use for good.

Does God always use man's evil for good? How about when the pain involves something as tragic as sexual abuse? Again, check the record. Tamar, a victim of incest, will forever be enshrined in the genealogy of Jesus Christ as a prime example of His grace (Matthew 1:3). What man intends for evil, God will always use for good.

Naomi became so bitter that she changed her name to Mara. She didn't know then that she would one day hold a baby to her breast. "The women living there said, 'Naomi has a son.' And they named him Obed" (Ruth 4:16-17). Do you know where we later encounter Obed and his grandson David? Jesus' geneology reveals this startling fact: His ancestors included "Obed the father of Jesse, and Jesse the father of King David" (Matthew 1:5-6). God used the painful circumstances of a woman named "Bitter" to produce the Savior of the world! What man intends for evil, God will always use for good.

**Forgiveness Is Understanding That God Will Use Those Who Hurt Us as His Means of Building Character into Our Lives (Hebrews 5:8)**
We can learn from bad examples as well as good. Whatever we experience in life will either make us bitter or better.

My experiences with my dad have molded me into a better father. I hope that my children will never experience the pain of a parent's rejection as I did. I work overtime at letting them know they have an immediate entree into my life at any time. Without question, I experience some of my happiest moments when I pick up the phone in my office and hear the 150 decibels of my son's voice as he shouts, "Hi, Dad!"

My background significantly influenced my career path. I have given the past 19 years of my life to young people. You see, as a teenager, my cries for help fell on deaf ears. I longed to have someone in my life who cared and understood. Now I attempt to be that someone to students whose cries for help might also fall on deaf ears.

My effectiveness as a youth pastor has been greatly enhanced by my own painful past, and through it I know how young people feel. I relate to their doubts, discouragements, depressions, and despair. Four years of college and three years of graduate school did not compare with the education I received by growing up in my home.

My convictions and values were formed and fashioned in the crucible of personal suffering. As fire purifies gold, so pain purifies us. Jesus learned obedience through what He suffered (Hebrews 5:8). So can we. My commitment to the sanctity of the home, the sacredness of marriage, the dignity of all human life, the authority of the Word of God, the Lordship of Jesus Christ, the priority of obedience over rebellion, and the essential importance of serving others can be traced directly to the conclusions I reached when my circumstances forced me to ask some tough questions about the inequities of life.

I discovered this paradox: those whom we consider

to be ruining our lives are in reality making the great-est contributions to our development as individuals. What a God we have who can take the shattered pieces of a broken life and weave them together into a beautiful tapestry for His purpose and His glory!

**Forgiveness Is Visualizing the Pain We Suffer as a Reminder of the Unresolved Conflicts in the Life of the One Who Hurt Us (Acts 7:59-60)**
"Guns don't kill people. People kill people." The war being waged over gun control has never been fiercer. Wherever you stand on this controversial issue, it reflects a fact that remains unchallenged: something is desperately wrong with the human race. Theolo-gians call it "depravity." The Bible states, "The heart is deceitful above all things and beyond cure. Who can understand it?" (Jeremiah 17:9) Consequently, people kill people, emotionally and physically.

We respond to the attacks of people in one of two ways. We can react by focusing on our pain and seek-ing retaliation. Or, we can use our hurts as a reminder that the people who have hurt us have very deep and unresolved conflicts in their own lives. They are merely living up to their depravity!

Jesus understood this: "But Jesus would not en-trust Himself to them . . . for *He knew what was in a man*" (John 2:24-25, emphasis mine). He exclaimed from the cross, "Father, forgive them, for *they do not know what they are doing*" (Luke 23:34, emphasis mine).

Stephen, as he was being murdered, cried out, "Lord, do not hold this sin against them" (Acts 7:60). The next verse is equally powerful: "And Saul was there, giving approval to his death" (Acts 8:1). One chapter later this same Saul—persecutor, murderer, and bounty hunter—dropped in the dust en route to Damascus and surrendered his life to Jesus Christ. What prompted the transformation of his hardened heart? No doubt the seeds were planted on that fateful day when Saul watched a dying man who focused his attention, not on his personal pain, but on his assassins' need.

**Forgiveness Is Refocusing Our Affections on the Heavenly Realm of Blessing Rather Than on the Earthly Realm of Suffering (Romans 8:23)**
Something is wrong with the human race. Something is also wrong with you and with me.

The flames of my commitment too easily flicker in the face of personal comfort. My passion for God peters out. My heart begins to attach itself to other things. Is this true of your life also?

Have you ever considered that personal pain is an antidote to this difficulty? Nothing shatters our attachments to things quicker than a good dose of suffering. Our world groans (Romans 8:22). Many times I groan too.

Put this epitaph on my tombstone: "Groaning inwardly I wait eagerly for Christ's return" (Romans 8:23). I long for that day when the trumpet sounds and Jesus Christ takes me to be with Himself. Thank God that He periodically allows the winds of adversity to blow my earthly attractions apart at the seams!

**Forgiveness Is Remembering That We Are in Spiritual Warfare (1 Timothy 1:18)**
We are targets. Satan seeks our total destruction. We pose a sizeable threat to his sinister schemes and he

will use whatever destructive devices he has at his disposal. Amazingly, his most powerful weapons of war often include our closest friends, associates, and loved ones.

Satan energized Peter in a feeble attempt to derail Christ's death (Matthew 16:23). He surrounded Paul with his blasphemous band. Paul lamented: "There are many who oppose me" (1 Corinthians 16:9). He made a prime target out of Timothy. "Alexander . . . did me a great deal of harm. You too should be on your guard against him" (2 Timothy 4:14-15).

Every assault sets the stage for potential defeat. Every aggression provides a golden opportunity for an attitude of bitterness to take root. Every attack, though Satanic is its origin, becomes human in its execution.

As the demons deployed their menacing missiles in an all-out effort to tear Timothy apart, Paul commanded his son in the faith to visualize the atrocities for what they were—the fallout of spiritual warfare (1 Timothy 1:18).

Peter was not Christ's enemy. Satan was. The many who opposed Paul were not his opponents. The demons who energized them were (1 Thessalonians 2:18). Alexander was not Timothy's primary foe. Paul recognized the real threat. "I was delivered from the lion's mouth" (2 Timothy 4:17; 1 Peter 5:8 refers to Satan as a roaring lion).

You are a target. The next time you experience a personal attack, remind yourself of the much bigger picture. Determine the identity of your real enemy. Rather than despise the one who is hurting you, intercede for him, asking God to break Satan's stranglehold in his life. Only as you take up this "shield of faith" will you successfully "extinguish all the flaming arrows of the evil one" (Ephesians 6:16).

### Forgiveness Is Reminding Ourselves That Bitterness Places Us in a Position Reserved Only for God (Romans 12:17-21)

Here's a valuable piece of insight: people become bitter because they choose to. Reread those last three words. No one can dictate your attitudes or mine. We choose them in every situation.

For over 20 years of my life I chose to feel bitter toward my dad. I never believed that my hatred was a matter of choice. I would have violently disagreed with such a proposition. But it was true. And I'll tell you why I chose to hate. Bitterness had become my feeble attempt at seeking revenge against my father.

What can you or I do when someone deals us a gut-wrenching blow? Physical force could result in a prison term. Property damage might generate a lawsuit. Our hands are basically tied. But our hearts are not!

In my life, bitterness made more sense than any other option—on the surface of things. If nothing else, I hoped to inflict upon my father the raw reality that his own son hated him and refused to allow him in his life. And so I fanned the flames.

The same sensations may have taken root in your own heart. Like a clenched fist, you have closed your heart against the one who hurt you. While such reactions are most understandable, they present a deadly threat to you.

God pierced my heart one day when I read these words:

Do not repay anyone evil for evil. Be careful to do what is right in the eyes of everybody. If it is possible, as far as it depends on you, live at peace with everyone. Do not take revenge, my friends, but leave room for God's wrath, for it is written: " 'It is mine to avenge; I will repay.' says the Lord." On the contrary: "If your enemy is hungry, feed him; if he is thirsty, give him something to drink. In doing this, you will heap burning coals on his head." Do not be overcome by evil, but overcome evil with good. (Romans 12:17-21)

The whole issue came down to one basic question: Did I want to relentlessly strike out at my dad or did I want God to control the situation? As long as I harbored bitterness, I effectively hindered God's ability to work in my dad's life. I needed to open that clenched fist of bitterness and allow God to intervene in His time and in His way. To state this principle simply, God did not give me, nor does He give you, the right of revenge. That right belongs to Him alone.

Words. Within the broad sweeping panorama of the English language, very few words stand alone. "Forgive" certainly belongs in that category. Now that you gained some significant new insights, let's apply them.

## In the Trenches:
## Waging Your Own War from Within

There's a lot more to the little seven-letter word "forgive" than meets the eye. How will you respond? What choices will you make? What changes will you allow to take place? To help you on your way, let me suggest the following:

1. Take a sheet of paper and write down from memory the facts that you have learned from this chapter.

2. Memorize the following verses to reinforce in your mind the definitions of forgiveness as we discussed them: Ephesians 4:32; Genesis 50:20; Hebrews 5:8; Acts 7:59-60; Romans 8:23; 1 Timothy 1:18; and Romans 12:19.

3. Ask yourself, "Who are the people in my life I need to forgive?"

4. Be honest with yourself. What is holding you back from forgiveness? What do you hope to gain by remaining bitter? Are you really hurting the person, or are you destroying yourself? What will it take to get you to open your clenched fist and allow God to take over?

5. Can you pinpoint a time in your life when you realized that you rebelled against an infinitely holy

God, deeply hurting and offending Him (Romans 3:23)? Did you admit that you can do absolutely nothing to make yourself acceptable to God (Matthew 5:48)? Have you invited Jesus Christ into your life to forgive you and take control of your life (John 1:12)?

Jesus Christ died for you. He shed His blood for you. On the cross He paid the penalty for your sins. If you have never committed your life to the Lord Jesus Christ, or if you're just not sure that you have, then why not settle this issue once and for all? Pray this prayer right now:

> Lord Jesus, I realize now that I desperately need You in my life. I admit that I have lived like a rebel and have deeply hurt and offended You. I am so ashamed of all the times that I have disobeyed You. Right now, in the best way I know, I invite You to come into my life to forgive my sins and to take control. Thank You that I have finally found the one relationship that I can count on forever. Thank You that You will never leave me or turn Your back on me. And thank You for Your promise that when I fail in the future, You will always be right there to pick me up, clean me off and keep me going. Help me now to live every day of my life for You.

If you prayed that prayer and meant it, Christ just performed in You the greatest miracle He's ever done. You just became a brand new person! (2 Corinthians 5:17) You have now experienced God's forgiveness. Before you even finished the prayer, He wiped your slate completely clean! (Romans 6:23)

And Christ is now preparing a place where you will live with Him forever! (John 14:1) Congratulations on making the most important decision you will ever make!

Having just experienced God's forgiveness, shouldn't you now forgive those who have hurt you? Jesus said, "If you hold anything against anyone, forgive him" (Mark 11:25).

# 4. The Moment of Truth

*Therefore, the kingdom of heaven is like a king who wanted to settle accounts with his servants. (Matthew 18:23)*

"I'm your stepmother."

"My what? My stepmother?" I thought to myself, "What is this lady talking about? I don't have a stepmother."

I've always hated surprises. If the shock wave of this unexpected encounter could have been measured on the Richter Scale the tremor would have set the all-time record. Somehow I sensed that, after this introduction, I would never be the same.

This unknown woman forced an issue I could not escape. Years of separation from my father abruptly ended in a moment of time. The choices I would be making in the next two hours would forever alter the course of the rest of my life.

Life can be reduced to a series of choices. And choices result in consequences, either good or bad. Admittedly, many choices are somewhat inconsequential. The destiny of the world hardly hinges upon which brand of toothpaste you decide to use in the morning. However, certain choices will dramatically affect the rest of your life, like it or not.

Over the years, I have faced a couple of such turning points. Let me tell you about one of them.

Our high school winter camp was in full swing. Saturday morning brought with it a thin layer of snow covering the grounds at Pine Summit, a beautiful facility nestled snugly in the San Bernardino Mountains, overlooking Big Bear Lake in southern California. We finished breakfast and started up the hill toward the chapel.

A woman drove into the camp. She parked her car, walked up to a staff person, and asked for Dewey Bertolini. I went over to the woman and introduced myself. She responded, "It's so good to meet you. I've heard so much about you. Dewey, I'm your stepmother."

"My what?" The reality began to sink in. My father had married this woman. For five years I had built a wall of separation between myself and my father and in one unexpected turn this strange woman successfully shattered the wall.

Confusion spread quickly through me like wildfire. Questions began to swirl through my mind. "What is she doing here? How did he find out where I was? What did they want from me now?" She must have sensed my hesitation because she continued, "Your father and I have been spending the weekend at a friend's cabin about two miles from here. He'd love to see you. Is there any way you can get away for a couple of hours?"

I was stunned! I felt as if someone had just punched me in the stomach. I thought to myself, "Get away? For a couple of hours? To see him? No way! Come on, lady, you've got to be kidding."

I became furious and was in the process of telling her where she could go—right back to her cabin—when five of my students surrounded me. The pressure within me was immense as each of the students had two eyeballs glued intently on me. One of them pulled on my shirt sleeve and asked, "What are you going to do Dewey—youth pastor, spiritual leader, model, example, the one after whose life we should pattern our own?"

### Eating Your Words Is a Good Thing to Do

I realized I had no choice. Reluctantly, I got into the car. Little did I know that by the time I returned to Pine Summit that afternoon, my world would have become completely upended.

The trip to the cabin seemed to take forever. The car became a cubicle of isolation. My mind reeled with terrifying thoughts: "What should I say? How should I act? What if I can't handle this? I'm just not ready. I've had no time to prepare. I saw him last as he was leaving the house with suitcase in hand. Has it been five years already?" I pinched myself, hoping that I would awaken from a nightmare. This simply couldn't be happening.

"We're here." Her words jarred me out of my silence. I could avoid the encounter no longer. I walked up the driveway, climbed a half-dozen stairs, turned the doorknob, stepped inside, and saw him. For the first time in five years our eyes met. He looked so old. And he appeared so frail. Had it only been five years? He looked as if he had aged 15. His hair had turned completely gray. He stood bent, his hands clutching the back of a chair. My one-time powerful, intimidating, abusive father now looked aged and weak. He lifted his right hand and reached out to take mine.

Believe me, I do not believe in out-of-body experiences, but on this occasion I felt as if I were a spectator rather than a participant, watching myself perform like an actor on a stage. I faced a monumental choice. My "turning point" had come.

Every sensation within me wanted me to scream profanity at him and walk out. After what seemed like hours, I slowly walked across the living room floor, faced my dad, lifted my right hand, and placed it in his.

When our hands joined together, I felt like a bathtub filled with stagnant water. Someone pulled the plug and every drop of the dirty liquid of my bitterness drained out. I no longer saw my dad as a tyrannical maniac bent on destroying my life, but as a desperately needy individual who hurt deeply inside. I viewed him as a lonely and angry man who tragically chose to strike out at the world, all the while alienating himself from those who were closest to him.

As we talked, the topic of my education and future goals came up. When I told him I was attending Talbot Seminary, preparing to become a preacher, his eyes lit up. He said to me, "You mean you're driving over 100 miles a day to get to school and back? Why don't you move in with me during the school year? I live only five minutes from your campus."

When God decides to move, He moves powerfully. One hour earlier I had harbored a root of bitterness toward my father, carefully cultivated for years. Now I was making plans to move in with him.

I needed to get back to the camp. Throughout the day my mind kept returning to my "chance" encounter with my father. Later that evening, in the privacy of my cabin, I began to read my Bible. I came to Matthew 18:21: "Then Peter came to Jesus and asked, 'Lord, how many times shall I forgive my brother when he sins against me? Up to seven times?' " Talk about having my bell rung. My entire situation suddenly came into focus. The first step in overcoming bitterness became crystal clear:

## Step One: You Must Be Willing to Forgive

Allow me to become personal for a moment. I stated the principle in the last chapter. I will develop it now. If you harbor bitterness toward someone, you do so for one simple reason. You choose to. Bitterness is primarily a matter of the will, not the emotions.

Perhaps you've heard the little Sunday School chorus, "Oh, How I Love Jesus." Someday I'd like to write a song with a slight variation: "Oh, How I Love Peter." Peter had no inhibitions; he let it all hang out. The so-called "apostle with the foot-shaped mouth" tipped his hand with his off-the-cuff query, "Lord, how many times do I have to forgive this guy? Isn't seven enough?" (my paraphrase)

Jesus' answer struck at the heart of the issue. "Peter, don't stop forgiving." The reason is this simple: the moment you stop forgiving, you start destroying.

Motivated by my desire for revenge, I chose to become bitter. My hate-filled response became the one means by which I could strike out at my father. I held within my grasp the potential of inflicting upon him the knowledge that his son had completely cut him out of his life. For years I operated on this principle.

You too may have become bitter for a similar reason. If so, you are in for a sad day of discovery for while you may think that you are destroying the one you hate, you are, in reality, only destroying yourself.

Handshakes can mean a variety of things. Handshakes express a common greeting between friends. Or handshakes can communicate the acceptance of a new acquaintance during a formal introduction. But some handshakes simply hide the real emotions of dislike or disdain one feels toward another.

I don't mask my feelings very well. When I shook my father's hand that morning, I was not acting hypocritically. That one gesture communicated volumes of truth. After years of planting, watering, and nurturing my harvest of hatred, I was now willing to allow God to change my heart.

Consider taking that same step right now. You may be carrying a huge burden God never intended you to carry. The time has come for you to get out of the way and let Him take over. "Do not repay evil for evil. Do not take revenge, my friends, but leave room for God's wrath. Do not be overcome by evil, but overcome evil with good" (Romans 12:17, 19, 21).

I suggest that you pray right now and admit to Him:

Father, I know that I have been wrong in harboring these feelings of bitterness. I know that by doing so I have been damaging myself while at the same time disobeying You. I cannot change my heart myself. Only You can do that. I am willing to have You replace my heart of hatred with a heart of love, in Your own time and in Your own way. Thank You for hearing and for answering my prayer.

How can you be sure that He heard you? Check out 1 John 5:14-15: "This is the assurance we have in approaching God: that if we ask anything according to His will He hears us. And if we know that He hears us—whatever we ask—we know that we have what we asked of Him." Be assured that God wants you to forgive the one who hurt you—up to seventy times seven. And be assured He not only heard you—He'll answer your prayer.

After coming to grips with the implications of Matthew 18:21 and 22, I continued reading. The next 14 verses charted the course my life was to take in the days immediately following my reunion with Dad.

Jesus dramatically illustrated the principles at hand with a powerful parable. The following summarizes the story.

A certain king decided to settle accounts with his slaves. One slave owed him $10 million. In those days a slave who did not have the means to pay his debt could find himself, along with his family, decaying in a debtor's dungeon. When threatened with this possibility, the slave fell on his knees and begged the king to forgive him. The king responded by canceling the debt and "let him go" (verse 27).

This same slave sought a fellow slave who owed him $18. He grabbed him, began to choke him, and demanded immediate payment of this insignificant amount. Not having $18, the fellow slave fell to his knees and begged for forgiveness.

If you had just been forgiven of a $10 million debt, what would you have done? If you can believe it, this ungrateful, self-centered slave rejected the pleas of his fellow slave and had the man thrown in prison until he could pay off his $18 debt.

> Then the master called the servant in. "You wicked servant," he said, "I canceled all that debt of yours [ten million dollars] because you begged me to. Shouldn't you have had mercy on your fellow servant just as I had on you?" In anger his master turned him over to the jailers until he should pay back all he owed. (Matthew 18:32-34)

Then Jesus added these ominous words: "This is how My heavenly Father will treat each of you unless you forgive your brother from your heart."

From this parable, the next step I needed to take became very obvious:

### Step Two: Make Two Lists

I put the Bible down, picked up a sheet of paper, and began listing everything my father ever did to deeply hurt and offend me. I included each incident I related in the first chapter, plus many more.

Then I created a second list. I listed everything I had ever done to deeply hurt and offend God. I recorded every act of rebellion I could remember. The first time I ever said the name, "Jesus Christ," I used it as a swear word. In rapid-fire succession, other mournful memories flashed through my mind. I chronicled them all, filling up page after page.

After completing my lists, I compared them. In one hand I held a list of things I had done to hurt and offend God—a $10-million list. In the other I held a list of things my father had done to hurt me—an $18 list.

And yet, years ago on one sultry summer evening in July 1969, in response to my sincere prayer to receive Jesus Christ, God had wiped the slate of my life completely clean. In essence, God took my $10 million debt and tore it up.

### Step Three: Tear Up Your First List

Next, I took the list of my father's offenses against me and tore it up. In effect, I wiped his slate completely clean. No, the memories of my father's abusive actions and cutting words did not disappear. The pain I carried for so long did not vanish. Yet I can honestly confess to you that I no longer hold these offenses against my father.

### Step Four: Make One More List

Based upon Joseph's words to his brothers in Genesis 50:20, "You intended to harm me, but God intended it for good," I made a list of every possible benefit that came to my life because God gave me the father that He did. As I began to ponder this, I found myself not only forgiving him, but thanking God for giving him to me. I chose to put 1 Thessalonians 5:18 into practice: "Give thanks in all circumstances, for this is God's will for you in Christ Jesus." Without this step the process of forgiveness will remain incomplete.

I hesitate to share my list because abusive fathers are far too commonplace in our society and I do not believe that it would be that helpful. Instead, let me share another true story with you.

A couple of years ago a girl in my college group was brutally raped. While getting into her car, "Judy" heard a twig snap behind her. A man jumped out from behind a bush, held a knife to her throat, threw her into the back of his van, drove her out to a deserted field, repeatedly raped her for hours, drove her back into the city, and, in her words, "threw me into the gutter like a wadded up piece of trash."

Her mother recounted for me this horrible succession of events. Understandably, Judy did not want to see me. Finally, at the request of her mother, I walked into her living room, only to find her lying on the couch in a fetal position, sobbing uncontrollably. She shouted at me, "You lied to me."

"What do you mean I lied to you?"

"You taught me that God is loving and powerful. If He is so loving and powerful, why was I raped?" I offered no answer for I had none.

For two hours I tried my best to comfort her. Near the end of our discussion, I asked her if she had ever stopped to consider whether any positive benefits had come to her because of her tragic ordeal.

She sneered at me. "You fairy-tale Christians! You're all the same. Positive benefits? You've got to be kidding!" I reasoned with her for a while longer and told her that I would return in a week. "I'd like to see your list when I come back," I said.

When I returned, Judy presented me with a list of

28 benefits that have come to her life because of her being raped. Some of these hard-to-believe blessings follow.

• "The man held a knife to my throat. He could have killed me. But he didn't. God protected my life. Now I know what the Psalmist meant when he prayed, 'Even when walking through the dark valley of death I will not be afraid, for you are close beside me, guarding, guiding all the way' " (Psalm 23:4, TLB).

• "Because of a throat infection I had been taking high doses of penicillin during the three weeks prior to my rape. The doctor in the emergency room told me that I do not need to fear any sexually transmitted disease since my body was flooded with the antibiotic. I thank God for that."

• "While riding in the back of the ambulance, en route to the hospital, the thought occurred to me, 'What if I'm pregnant?' I have always regarded abortion as murder. Now I faced the real possibility. I determined that if I were pregnant there was no way I would kill a human life that God had created. One of my convictions was tested and I passed the test! Gratefully, I learned later I had not conceived."

• "I now have a fear of men. I'm even afraid to date. I wondered if this fear would carry over into my marriage. Then I read 1 John 4:18: 'But perfect love drives out fear.' I am now confident that when I meet the man God intends for me to marry, I will have no fear."

• "After studying about sexual abuse I discovered that one out of four girls and one out of five guys will be sexually abused before they reach the age of 18. I have decided to dedicate my life to helping the victims of sexual abuse. I have thought of opening up a halfway house some day."

• "The doctor in the emergency room the night of my rape was a Christian. God knew that I desperately needed spiritual and emotional help in addition to physical help. He was faithful and provided it."

• "I have learned the importance of obeying my parents. For some reason they told me not to go to my friend's house the night I was attacked. They really felt strongly about it. They couldn't give me any concrete reasons, so I went anyway. Now I know that God was using them to warn me. I'll never disobey them again!"

• "The newspaper carried the story and I was humiliated. Twenty-five thousand families in my city read about me being raped. But the last paragraph told about my faith in Christ and how He sustained me during the ordeal. Can you believe it? God used my story to influence the whole community for Him."

• "I recalled reading about Paul's 'thorn in the flesh.' God told him, 'My grace is sufficient for you, for My power is made perfect in weakness' (2 Corinthians 12:9). I now realize that the very thing I feared would destroy my life, God will use the most to express His power through my life."

• "I thank God that I am still a virgin. I learned something about purity through this awful experience. Purity can never be taken away; purity can only be given away. Purity is a matter of the heart. There is no way a madman with a knife can touch the inner part of me. I am as pure as newly fallen snow."

Over the years I have spoken face-to-face with hundreds of girls and guys who have suffered the indignity of incest, molestation, or rape. Without exception, every young person to whom I have spoken has blamed himself or herself. The personal guilt they carry has made the emotional scars that much deeper. I have used Judy's story across this country and throughout Canada as a powerful testimony to the fact that victims of sexual abuse or assault are not guilty. God said, in reference to rape: "Only the man who has done this shall die. Do nothing to the girl; she has committed no sin" (Deuteronomy 22:25-26). I have seen so many young people shed tears of joy as God's Spirit used His Word and Judy's testimony as His means of setting these poor emotional captives free (John 8:32).

## Step Five: Understand That the Healing Process Takes Time

As the song says, "We've only just begun." No one expects years of emotional trauma and deeply ingrained behavior patterns of hatred to vanish overnight. There is no substitute for time.

No one can tell you how long the process will take. I can tell you that five years transpired between "the handshake" and my complete healing. During those five years God rebuilt a relationship that I had written off as forever fractured and hopelessly broken. My dad and I ended up as best friends. I probably would not have believed it were possible had I not lived it. I experienced the principle firsthand, "For nothing is impossible with God" (Luke 1:37).

The story did not end in that little cabin tucked away in a corner of Pine Summit. More questions needed to be answered. You might be wondering, "What steps did you take during those five intervening years to heal your relationship? Does the Bible offer any insight into the restoration process? Can I be certain that my situation can also be healed?" I will answer these questions, and many more, in the next chapter.

### In the Trenches:
### Waging Your Own War from Within

1. Have you honestly faced the questions, "Am I willing to allow God to change my heart? Am I willing to forgive _____ ?" If not, consider doing so now.

I know that you may have strong doubts and fears. You may be dealing with questions like these: "What if things don't change? What if I continue to hate him?" I suggest that you don't allow yourself to be held prisoner by such doubts. You will probably stumble and fall many times along the way. Remember, forgiveness is a process. We're not talking about a light switch that you turn on or off. We're talking about a dimmer switch that comes on gradually. Begin right now. Confess to God your willingness to have Him change your heart. Express to Him as well the doubts and concerns that you feel.

2. Are you prepared to make a couple of lists? Take this step when you have some time to think.

Recalling some of these memories will no doubt be painful, but necessary. There is something therapeutic about facing your hurts honestly. Remember that living in a state of denial will only compound the problem. After making your lists, read Matthew 18:21-35. Which of your lists is a $10-million list? Which is the $18 list? After you have considered the parable in Matthew 18, tear up the $18 list!

3. Have you considered the positive benefits that

have come to your life because of the offenses you
have experienced? Give this one a lot of thought. Ask
God to enable you to see the situation from His perspective. Claim the promise of James 1:2-5:

> Consider it pure joy, my brothers, whenever
> you face trials of many kinds, because you know
> that the testing of your faith develops persever-
> ance. Perseverance must finish its work so that
> you may be mature and complete, not lacking
> anything. If any of you lacks wisdom [the ability
> to see a situation in the same way that God
> does], he should ask God, who gives generously
> to all without finding fault, and it will be given
> to him.

4. Allow time for the process to take effect. Don't sit
idly by during this period. This time of healing will
allow you to apply a number of principles I will out-
line in the next chapter.

# 5. IT AIN'T OVER
# TILL IT'S OVER

*On the contrary: "If your enemy is hungry, feed him; if he is thirsty, give him something to drink. In doing this, you will heap burning coals on his head." (Romans 12:20)*

The memo read, "Report to the dean's office immediately."

On impulse I thought to myself, "What did I do now?" It could only mean trouble. Why else would the dean of men at Talbot Seminary pull me out of my New Testament Introduction class?

He met me in the hallway, put his hand on my shoulder, and tried to break the news as calmly as possible. "We've just received an emergency phone call from your stepmother. Your father has suffered a serious heart attack and has been rushed into emergency surgery at Huntington Memorial Hospital."

The drive from Talbot to the hospital should normally take 45 minutes; I made it in 20. I ran into the lobby, demanded directions of an attendant, and rushed into the cardiac care waiting room.

The mood in the room was somber. Every person there was awaiting the news concerning a loved one. Some would be comforted by a doctor's prognosis; others would be devastated by a less positive report. Some people read, others cried softly, while still others helplessly stared off into space.

The hours ticked by. "What's taking so long?" I asked pleadingly. The nurses simply shrugged their shoulders and responded with a blank stare. Nobody would talk to me.

Suddenly everything seemed to happen at once. My stepmother arrived and filled me in. "I was in the kitchen when I heard a muffled cry from the bedroom. I ran in and there he was on the floor, face down." She trembled as she held the back the tears.

Our conversation was cut short by the doctor.

"Mrs. Bertolini? Would you please join me over here?" We braced ourselves for the worst. He was concise and to the point. "Your husband suffered a heart attack. He has sustained significant damage requiring us to perform triple bypass surgery, taking pieces of an artery from his leg and patching them over the damaged portion of his heart. The next few days will be critical. You can see him in the recovery room, but only for a few minutes."

My stepmother can handle most anything. And so I was surprised when she needed help out of the recovery room.

"It's your turn," one of them said to me. I glanced over at the limp figure of my stepmom as she lay on one of the couches, braced myself, and walked in.

Words cannot do justice to the scene that I was about to observe. A strange silence permeated the room. Only the low hum from a piece of life-support apparatus, and an erratic, pulsating buzz from my dad's heart monitor made any sound. There were tubes everywhere (it seemed like hundreds), plugged into every imaginable opening in my dad's seemingly lifeless body. He looked like he was caught in the grasp of an alien being's tentacles. A video camera provided around the clock observation.

As I approached the stainless steel gurney onto which my dad was strapped, I noted the massive bandages over his chest. Orange antiseptic covered him from the neck down. His skin was gray and his eyes were closed. His body lay absolutely still. I could detect no breathing, and apart from the erratic buzz of the pulsating monitor, I would have thought that I was looking at a corpse.

I stayed for what seemed like hours. Yet, after only a few minutes, a polite attendant asked me to leave. I reluctantly complied with his request.

The next morning, my dad was moved to the cardiac care unit. I walked into a clinical cavern of medical machinery, augmented by blinking lights and haunting sounds, complete with a spider's web of hoses and wires.

As my shadow passed over his eyes, I noticed him flinch, ever so slightly. He attempted to clear the phlegm from his throat. He sensed that someone was standing next to him. His lips quivered as he asked for water. I buzzed for the nurse. She dipped a Q-Tip into a glass of water, and forced it into my dad's dry mouth.

Dad managed to open his eyes a bit wider. I could see his pupils adjusting to the light in the room as he tried to focus.

He recognized me. His hand began to inch its way along the rail to the nurse's call button. As he did so his heart monitor began to beat faster and more erratically. He pushed the button and within seconds the nurse appeared.

Panic seized me. I was afraid my presence was somehow worsening the situation. Nurses surrounded his bed, poised for action. Dad parted his lips and began to speak in a barely audible voice. The nurses bent over to place their ears near his mouth to listen. I stared in silence. The room began to grow hazy. Time seemed to stand still.

How had my dad and I gotten here? Was this man really the object of my hatred for so many years? My mind began to replay memories. Five years had come and gone since that fateful "handshake." It seemed like only yesterday that his wife had introduced herself to me as my stepmother. Where had the time gone?

Precious memories my dad and I held in common had developed over that five-year period. During that time I had watched in awe as God repaired a hopelessly broken relationship.

My dad wheezed. Once again my attention was riveted on his emaciated figure. I bent down to hear his whisper. In a muffled gurgle, my father uttered four words—words I had waited 23 years to hear.

As I stood, clinging to the rail of my father's bed, I looked into the face of the man who had become my best friend. I wondered what had brought us to this place.

The steps I listed in the last chapter constituted only the beginning in the process of reconciliation. A long, arduous road remained before me. With the Bible as my guide, I discovered five more principles absolutely essential to completing the process.

## Do Not Expect the Other Person to Change

Forgiveness should place no expectations on the one forgiven. If you entertain the thought, "I've changed my heart. Now you'd better change yours," you may be setting yourself up for disappointment. The other person's failure to change will only cause you to re-kindle your bitterness once again.

Like so many other things in life, I had to learn this principle the hard way. I had refused to accept the humanity of my father. He was not created a comput-er and I could not program him according to my de-sired responses. He had needs, hurts, and conflicts in his life just as I had. Some ran very deep; many, in fact, he had harbored for years. His abrasive manner became an outward expression of his inward pain.

I remember another meeting in a different hospital where I learned that, just as I had to allow myself the time needed to heal, I needed to allow my dad the necessary time to heal.

The scene took place in the maternity ward of the Glendale Memorial Hospital. After 90 minutes of la-bor, my wife delivered our first child. In an earsplit-ting, blood-curdling scream, our little David let the world know he had arrived. My dad rushed to the hospital, anxiously anticipating the first glimpse of his first grandchild.

Upon his arrival, he raced up to the huge plate glass window and peered into the nursery. The atmosphere in that hallway felt electric as parents, grandparents, sisters and brothers alike gazed at their newborns with obvious pride. The corridor was jammed full of love-filled people.

My father took one look at David and thundered cynically, "Well, Dewey, you finally did something right." Every eye turned in my direction. I was totally humiliated. My father hadn't changed. He couldn't even offer a compliment without lacing it with cynical barbs.

How should I have responded? I felt like exploding, striking back with anger—fighting fire with fire. But for whatever reason, on this occasion, I didn't. I looked past my pain and embarrassment and into my dad's heart to find the source of his attack. Do you know what I saw? I saw a man who believed deep within that he could do nothing right.

I responded to him by asking, "What do you think of your grandson, Dad?" We went on in a fairly normal way to celebrate one of the most memorable nights of our lives, because I was beginning to accept that my father might never change.

You might be asking, "But if I can change, why can't he?" Consider these three reasons:

(1) You and I have no control over the actions and attitudes of another. We have control only over our own. For this reason, Paul commanded: "If it is possible, *as far as it depends on you,* live at peace with everyone" (Romans 12:18, emphasis mine).

(2) Only God can change a heart. Yet, a person may resist God's working in his life. Consequently, he may end up hardening his heart, while entrench-

ing himself more deeply in his offensive attitudes in the process.

(3) God wants to use our painful experiences to build Christlike character (love, joy, peace, patience, kindness, goodness, faithfulness, gentleness, and self-control [Galatians 5:22]) into our lives. God may decide to use human hammers and chisels to skillfully cut away at our rough edges. Unfortunately, extensive chiseling may be necessary before He can produce in us His desired results.

I hope you do not get the impression that after "the handshake" I became the model of sinless perfection as I interacted with my father. Many months transpired before I was able to summon the courage to react as I did in that corridor of the maternity ward. You too will no doubt struggle as you reach for a mature response to the person who has hurt you. But the victory begins when you and I accept the fact that the person who has offended us so deeply may never change.

## Distinguish Between Your Responsibilities and Your Concerns

One of my students recently approached me with this problem: "Dewey, this Sunday night I am going to preach my very first sermon ever and I need your help. Every time I sit at my desk to prepare my message, this thought keeps running through my mind: 'You're a hypocrite. How can you preach a message of love to others when you hate your own father?' "

He had a valid point. I said to him, "You're right. You can't expect to preach with any power until your attitudes are changed." Then I led him through the steps we discussed in chapter 4. He wept as he realized the magnitude of his hatred. He displayed genuine remorse as he asked God to cleanse him.

One week later we got together. He told me that when he preached on Sunday night he felt a freedom he never before experienced. He had genuinely forgiven his dad. He then asked me about a different, but related, problem.

"What do I do about my mother? My dad harasses her continuously. He's going to emotionally destroy her if he doesn't stop. Every time he treats her that way I feel a rage inside of me. What should I do?"

I hear similar stories every week. I am deeply frustrated at times because these are the toughest situations to face. As much as my dad hurt me, I experienced an even greater pain when I watched him abuse my mother and sisters.

My student understood this also. Forgiveness came relatively easily when he thought about his own pain. But forgiving his dad for the pain inflicted upon his mother was quite another story.

I outlined my answer as follows:

(1) "You cannot fight your mother's battles. Only she can do that. When God said: 'My grace is sufficient for you, for my power is made perfect in weakness' (2 Corinthians 12:9), he made the promise to Paul, not to everyone who stood by watching Paul suffer. God will give your mother His grace to turn her weaknesses into an expression of His power just as He supplied that grace to you. But He won't give you the grace to fight her battles for her.

(2) "You cannot become your mother's guardian. Only God can do that. His promise to her stands sure: 'God is faithful; He will not let you be tempted

(the Greek word can also be translated "tested") beyond what you can bear. But when you are tempted (or tested), He will also provide a way out so that you can stand up under it' (1 Corinthians 10:13).

(3) "You can support your mother. Along with your prayers, you can provide for her some things that perhaps no one else can—a listening ear, a shoulder to cry on, a sensitive and compassionate spirit, and a calming voice of hope.

(4) "You can offer counsel when asked. Your mom needs someone to turn to for advice. Rather than expending emotional energy against your father because of what he's doing to her, channel your energy into finding biblical solutions to her questions so that you'll 'always be prepared to give an answer to everyone who asks you to give the reason for the hope that you have. But do this with gentleness and respect' (1 Peter 3:15-16).

(5) "Don't take sides. Joining hands with your mother against your father will only rob you of future opportunities to influence your dad.

(6) "You must allow God to work in your mother's life through her own pain. I know that you would like to alleviate your mother's suffering. But doing so ahead of God's schedule could short circuit the character building process that God has designed for her.

(7) "You must guard your own heart against bitterness. If you don't, you may forfeit the privilege of ever helping anyone."

## Find Creative Ways to Become a Servant

Have you ever done a character study of the 12 apostles? Talk about a hodgepodge of personalities—Jesus had a traveling road-show on His hands! I am sure that on many occasions Jesus felt like shaking His head while saying to Himself, "Why Me?"

Look, for instance, at Luke 9. An internal eruption threatened to splinter the unity of the group. "An argument started among the disicples as to which of them would be the greatest" (verse 46). Jesus rebuked them by stating one of the all-time secrets to healing broken relationships: "If anyone wants to be first, he must be the very last, and the servant of all" (Mark 9:35).

Serving involves identifying and creatively trying to meet the needs in another person's life, regardless of the personal sacrifice involved. It involves equal obedience to Paul's command in Romans 12:20: "Instead, feed your enemy if he is hungry. If he is thirsty give him something to drink and you will be 'heaping coals of fire on his head.' In other words, he will feel ashamed of himself for what he has done to you" (TLB).

The compilers of *The Life Application Bible* write:

> In this day of constant lawsuits and incessant demands for legal rights, Paul's command sounds almost impossible. When someone hurts you deeply, instead of giving him what he deserves, Paul says to befriend him. Why does Paul tell us to forgive our enemies? (1) Forgiveness may break a cycle of retaliation and lead to mutual reconciliation. (2) It may make the enemy feel ashamed and change his ways. (3) By contrast, returning evil for evil hurts you just as much as it hurts your enemy. Even if your enemy never repents, forgiving him will free you of a heavy load of bitterness.[1]

My father's recovery from open heart surgery presented me with a golden opportunity to put this verse into practice. He could no longer mow his lawn, so every week I voluntarily mowed it for him. Several rooms in his house needed paint; I grabbed a brush and ladder and went to work. A black, slimy substance started growing on the tile in the shower. With a bottle of cleaner in hand, I declared war against that fungal intruder, and presented to my father the cleanest shower on the block. Nothing endeared me more to my dad than these self-initiated acts of service.

### If the One Who Offended You Is Your Parent, Apply the Principles of Obedience and Honor

Paul clearly states this principle in Ephesians 6:1-2: "Children, obey your parents in the Lord, for this is right. Honor your father and mother." It is important to distinguish between the key terms. Obedience refers to an action; honor refers to an attitude. Obedience can be defined simply as "doing what we are asked to do, when we are asked to do it." Honor goes one step beyond obedience. Honor demands that we treat our parents with the same respect with which we would treat Jesus Christ in our homes.

I'll be the first to admit that many parents do not deserve this kind of respect. Children can see through hypocrisy faster than anyone. Many young people conclude that, because of their parents' inconsistencies, they do not need to show them respect. Rebellion often becomes their most powerful means of protest.

Such an attitude fails to acknowledge one very important principle: while the person may not deserve such respect, the position as a parent certainly does. For example, Richard Nixon resigned from the office of the Presidency because he faced certain impeachment. Many did not regard him as worthy of holding the highest office in the land. Yet, until the day he resigned, even his loudest critics addressed him as "Mr. President." While, because of illegal activities, the person did not deserve respect, the office he held certainly did.

David properly applied this principle when he refused to show disrespect to a homicidal king. He correctly discerned the difference between Saul's person and position when he said: "The LORD forbid that I should do such a thing to my master, the LORD's annointed, or lift my hand against him; for he is the anointed of the LORD" (1 Samuel 24:6).

If my father were only one of 5.2 billion people walking on the planet, unrelated to me in any way, he might not have deserved my respect. But he wasn't only one of 5.2 billion. He held a position in my life that was unique to me. He was my father, and as such, deserved to be respected.

Are we ever justified in disobeying our parents? Yes, when they ask us to violate the clear teaching of the Word of God. At that point, we may respectfully choose to obey God rather than man (Acts 4:19).

## Do Not Overly Concern Yourself with Your Feelings

You may not feel like doing any of this. Feelings of anger may still consume you. You may resent the fact that the other person has not changed. You may want to strike out at someone because of what he did to a loved one. You may detest the thought of serving someone who hurt you so deeply. Rebellious acts may fill your fantasies.

I do not place a lot of stock in emotions, for two reasons: (1) we cannot control them, and (2) God does not command us concerning them. Remember, forgiveness is a matter of our will, not our feelings. Forgiveness is volitional, not emotional.

In my experience with my father, I discovered that as long as I was doing what I knew to be right, my feelings eventually caught up with me and fell in line. Consider this excerpt from *The Life Application Bible:*

> Forgiveness involves both attitudes and action. If you find it hard to feel forgiving of someone who has hurt you, try acting forgiving. If appropriate, tell this person you would like to heal your relationship. Give him a helping hand. Send him a gift. Smile at him. Many times you will discover that *right actions lead to right feelings* (emphasis mine).[2]

In the Cardiac Care Unit, the nurses strained to hear my father's words. His lips quivered as he tried desperately to clear his throat. He finally managed to utter four words, not particularly meaningful to the nurses, but significant beyond description to me. He whispered, "This is my son."

He then heaved a great sigh. Very deliberately, he inched his hand along the bed rail and placed it upon mine, squeezing it slightly. Even though the pain must have been great, he mustered enough strength to make one more statement. He sighed once again, cleared his throat, and began to speak.

Now, I honestly don't know if the nurses noticed it

or not. But I did. In spite of his pain, Dad had a twinkle in his eyes. Despite his brush with death, his lips curled into a smile. Underneath his bandages, I could see him push his chest out, if only a little bit. He squeezed my hand once again, took a deep breath, and wheezed, "This is my son. He's a preacher!"

Again, I felt him squeeze my hand. Then his body went limp and his heart rate slowed. The buzz of the monitor shifted into a regular beat. The nurses politely straightened his pillow, adjusted his blankets, and left the room.

They had no idea of the drama that had just taken place. I had waited 23 years for that moment. For the first time in my life I knew my father felt proud of me! My dream of a lifetime had come true in that Cardiac Care Unit of the Huntington Memorial Hospital.

My dad fully recovered from his surgery and the healing of our relationship eventually was completed. If you had seen us going for walks around the neighborhood or taking in a Dodger game, you would have seen two best friends at play. But it came with much effort and sacrifice. It's true that the value of something is measured by the effort required in obtaining it. That being so, the relationship with my father became quite valuable indeed!

**In the Trenches:**
**Waging Your Own War from Within**

1. Turn back to chapter 3 and review the seven definitions of forgiveness. The motivation for taking the
five steps that I developed in this chapter flows out of
an understanding of forgiveness. Based upon those
definitions, can you honestly thank God for allowing
your situation to take place?

2. Are you attaching any expectations to your forgiveness? Are you willing to accept the fact that the
person who hurt you may never change? Will you be
patient in allowing God to change the person's heart
in His own time and in His own way?

3. Have you become bitter because of someone
else's pain? Are you viewing yourself as his protector
or savior? Do you feel frustrated because you seem
powerless to intervene? Turn these frustrations into
motivations to pray for the person. Do not pray that
God will change the situation. Pray that God will
change the people involved.

When faced with potential persecution that might
have resulted in prison or death, the followers of
Christ did not pray that the persecution would end.
They prayed for boldness in the midst of the persecution (Acts 4:23-31). They prayed for God to change,
not their circumstances, but their hearts.

We violate this most important principle when we
pray for God to remove our painful circumstances.
God always places His priority of character develop-

ment above our desire for creature comforts. God can only change situations as He changes peoples' hearts. Therefore, whenever you feel frustrated or angry, ask God to accomplish His purposes in and through the lives of the people involved, for His glory and for your ultimate good (Romans 8:28-29).

4.  Begin to look for ways in which you can become a servant to the one who hurt you. And as you perform your acts of kindness, do so with no strings attached.

Remember the words of our Lord Jesus: "Then the righteous will answer Him, 'Lord, when did we see You hungry and feed You, or thirsty and give You something to drink? When did we see You as a stranger and invite You in, or needing clothes and clothe You? When did we see You sick or in prison and go to visit You?

"The King will reply, 'I tell you the truth, whatever you did for one of the least of these brothers of mine, you did for Me' " (Matthew 25:37-40).

You may not desire to do anything for the one who offended you. In fact, you may feel nauseated at the thought. Your actions may go unheeded or unrecognized. No appreciation may be forthcoming. You may even be mocked and ridiculed along the way. However, in the ultimate sense, you are not only serving the one who hurt you, you are serving the Lord. He will not leave your effort unrecognized or unrewarded.

5.  If your parents are involved, review the section regarding obedience and honor. Remind yourself of the distinction between respect for the person versus

respect for the position. And if you have been bitter toward an employer, recognize that these same principles apply to your situation (Colossians 3:22-24).

6. Finally, ignore your negative feelings. Learn to live your life by your head rather than your heart. Emotions are fickle; they can change like the weather. Emotions are tricky; they can easily fool you. Emotions are not trustworthy; they are often just plain wrong. Do what you know to be right, and in time your feelings will catch up.

# 6. A PERMANENT ENDING

*When Jesus saw her weeping, and the Jews who had come along with her also weeping, He was deeply moved in spirit and troubled. "Where have you laid him?" He asked. "Come and see, Lord," they replied. Jesus wept. Then the Jews said, "See how He loved him." (John 11:33-36)*

Have you ever watched the stunt man in the circus trying frantically to spin 100 plates on 100 poles? On more than one occasion I have watched him make a mad dash from one rod to another, doing whatever he could to keep a single plate from falling.

Every time I walk past our telephone receptionist at The Master's College, I think of that man in the circus. Calls come pouring in to her switchboard at an unbelievable rate. Her ability to field all of those calls, placing some on hold and transferring others, rivals any juggling act in any circus anywhere. She ensures that my communication link with the outside world is secure.

My dependence upon her was exemplified on a chilly Tuesday afternoon in January 1985. I was talking to two students in the parking lot, when a girl ran up to me with the look of terror in her eyes. "Call the switchboard. There's an emergency message for you." I ran to my office, dialed the receptionist, and she connected me to my mother.

Mom was crying. "Can you get down here right away? There's been a terrible accident. Your dad's been hurt." Her voice trailed off.

"Hello," I yelled into the receiver. "Mom!" I heard a *click* and the *buzz* of the dial tone.

On the way to her home, I thought about my mother's tears. Even though the divorce had taken place several years earlier, she continued to have a deep emotional attachment to my father. My mom and stepmother had become extremely good friends. We had all become a unified family. Now we faced the tidal wave of an unexpected tragedy.

Within 15 minutes I picked Mom up and we headed south to the Huntington Memorial Hospital. When I entered the lobby, I experienced a classic case of deja vous. How long had it been since I was last here? Ten years? Twelve years? Time coalesced into a blur.

"Oh, Dewey, thank God you're here," my stepmother yelled as she came running to meet us. I took one look at the expression on her face, and I knew that something serious had happened. She grabbed my mother and me, took us into a corner of the lobby, and proceeded to describe a tragic scene of horror. "Your dad was driving on the freeway when he apparently passed out. The paramedics found him sprawled out on the ground." She couldn't continue.

Impulsively, I jumped out of my chair, ran into the emergency room, grabbed an orderly, and screamed, "Where's my father? I want to see my father." He led me into an office, no bigger than a broom closet, summoned a doctor, and instructed me to wait. Within a minute, a doctor walked in and introduced himself. His face and voice showed little emotion. His calloused, clinical coldness betrayed his indifference to the entire situation. "Your father is dead," he said coldly.

There is an awesome finality to the word "dead." It conveys an emptiness and hopelessness. It hit me with the full force of an atom bomb.

"What do you mean, 'dead?' " I asked him.

"We found your father lying in the street. I can assure you we tried everything we could to revive him. He must have known something was wrong because he managed to pull his car off the freeway. We surmise that he lost consciousness on the off-ramp and hit a chain-link fence. The force of the impact wrenched the door on the driver's side open, and your dad was catapulted out of the car and onto the pavement." He led me into one of the emergency rooms. "He's over there behind that curtain. If you have any questions, ask one of the nurses." And with those words he left. I suddenly felt incredibly alone.

I braced myself and grasped the edge of the curtain to pull it back. It wasn't like the last time I had seen him in a hospital room. There were no tubes. I heard no erratic buzz from the blinking pulse monitor. No video camera was positioned from the wall. Nor was there any cavern of equipment present. There was only a table and my father. He just lay there — and the raw reality began to sink in.

## Memories . . .

You've heard about those times when a person's life flashes before his eyes? That's exactly what happened to me. Momentarily I became transfixed as the emergency room transformed itself into a time tunnel. Memories of events and experiences, long since buried in my subconscious, began to emerge with unusual reality. In my imagination my dad sprang back to life. It was a precious time of remembrance.

I remembered the evening my stepmother went shopping, leaving my dad and me home together. Typically I studied throughout the afternoon. My dad and I would eat dinner together and watch a ball game or the evening news. Then I would hit the books again. But on this particular evening, my stepmom was gone and all was quiet.

Something had been bothering me deeply for several weeks. I needed to resolve it, but didn't know exactly what to do. I knew that I had forgiven my father. But I also knew that as much as my dad had hurt me, I too had hurt him. I needed to ask for his forgiveness.

I tried to rationalize the guilt away by thinking it was his fault. I told myself I wouldn't have cut him out of my life if he hadn't hurt me so deeply. But my feeble efforts at self-justification did little to calm my conscience. Then I remembered reading Jesus' words in Matthew 5:23-24: "Therefore, if you are offering your gift at the altar and there remember that your brother has something against you, leave your gift there in front of the altar. First go and be reconciled to your brother; then come and offer your gift." Every time I tried to read my Bible or pray, these words would torment me. "Leave your gift . . . and be reconciled."

I argued with myself. "He surely has nothing against me," I thought. "If he did, he would have told me. We're getting along just great, don't rock the boat. And besides, he has never really asked me to forgive him. Why should I have to ask him to forgive me?" I tried to forget the whole thing, but a gentle whisper kept nagging me. I couldn't escape the fact that I was responsible in several ways for the state of our relationship.

- I failed to show my dad any love when I was growing up;
- I failed to obey him. Rebellion characterized my mode of protest;
- I failed to honor him as my father;
- I purposely cut him out of my life, rejecting his every attempt to contact me;
- I harbored a root of bitterness against my father for years;
- I fantasized repeatedly about destroying him;
- I prayed that God would kill him on the spot;
- I denied him any hope of a positive father-son relationship.

It was no use. I couldn't study. I put my book down, walked into the living room, and looked at my father.

"I need to talk to you," I stammered. "I've been thinking about the last several years and I am ashamed about the way I've treated you. I haven't shown you the love and respect that you deserve as a father. I'd like to ask you to forgive me."

The next moment seemed like an eternity. He said nothing. Then he slowly rose from his chair, walked toward me, and threw his arms around me. For the first time in my life I saw my father cry.

### A Final Farewell

"Here you are." My mother's words shattered the silence of the hospital emergency room and jolted me out of my daydream. "We've been looking all over for you." Then she saw him. "Oh, my God," she cried and broke into tears.

Unless you have experienced the loss of a loved one, you can't have any comprehension of the myriad of details that must be worked out. We had to think about the funeral arrangements, notifying of friends and family, answering questions from the Highway Patrol, and so on. All of this in the midst of unbearable emotional turmoil.

The public viewing was held three days later. I couldn't go. I simply did not have enough emotional energy to bear the sight of my father's body again. I wanted to retreat into the lingering memories of the life we shared together, rather than walk away with the lasting impressions of a lifeless corpse. To this day, I still have not returned to his burial site. Perhaps someday.

The funeral itself served as a fitting tribute to the memory of my father. I stood bravely as the pall bearers carried his flag-draped coffin into the sanctuary. The flag signified that my father had served in the Navy during World War II, and I felt proud at the thought that he had risked his life as he fought for freedom.

A cacophony of weeping filled the air as my father's best friend read the eulogy. A myriad of disjointed thoughts bombarded my mind as I looked back on my dad's life. I recalled the night he walked into my bedroom and told me that he wanted to share some of my hobbies with me. "Do you think we could start doing some things together?" he asked.

I thought about the first time he came to hear me preach. After my message, I introduced my father to the congregation and had him stand. The church spontaneously broke into applause and everyone rose to their feet in a standing ovation.

In my mind, I replayed the memory of my father weeping like a baby as he watched my wedding ceremony. I'll never forget the way he beamed when he shook my hand and kissed my bride.

As I stood now at the graveside, I silently wondered to myself, "If my dad had the presence of mind to pull off the freeway, could he not have also had the presence of mind to cry out to Jesus Christ?" He certainly knew what was involved, for we had talked about it on numerous occasions. He would say to me, "I'd give anything to believe the way you do. I'm just not ready." Did he find himself ready before crashing into the chain link fence? I cling to that hope.

A contrast of emotions flooded my being as I bade a final farewell to my father. The sorrow of the moment was too intense to describe. Jesus understood. He, too, wept at the graveside of His departed friend (John 11:35). And yet, a joy seemed to permeate my soul. A joy that resulted from the fact that, if nothing else, my father went to his grave knowing that his son loved him. I whispered a final prayer before leaving that grassy knoll on which his casket lay, "Dear Father, thank You for allowing me to make things right with my dad before it was too late."

## In the Trenches:
## Waging Your Own War from Within

1. As I relived for you some of my special memories concerning my father, can you think of any happy times that you have shared with the one who hurt you? If so, train your mind to emphasize those pleasant memories while minimizing the painful ones.

If not, consider the fact that every memory shared in this chapter came after "the handshake." It wasn't until I began to restore my relationship with my father that this catalog of good times could be written. Be encouraged. Purpose in your own heart that once the initial steps in the forgiveness process have been taken, you too will begin to chronicle your own record of positive memories.

2. Is there anyone in your life about whom you can say, "Help me, God, to make things right before it is too late?" What steps are you going to take beginning today to "make things right?"

3. You might be thinking, "But what do I do if it is already too late?" I'll answer that question and many others in the final chapter.

# 7. I'M GLAD YOU ASKED

*As his custom was, Paul went into the synagogue, and on three Sabbath days he reasoned with them from the Scriptures. (Acts 17:2)*

Teaching has become an interesting way for me to earn a living. I've been at it long enough to know that as hard as I try to resolve an issue every time I speak, I usually succeed in raising more questions than I answer. This fact also applies to the topic of bitterness.

As you read this book, did you ever find yourself wishing you could verbalize a question to the author? I have taught on this subject for enough years to know that inquiries come fast and furious.

In light of this fact, I've considered how I should

**105**

best draw my thoughts to conclusion. Ideally, I'd like to sit down with you one-on-one and discuss your unique situation. Since this is not possible, I have opted for a question-and-answer format and have tried to cover a typical sampling of the kinds of questions I routinely receive.

**Question:** "Will my pain ever go away?"

**Answer:** Probably not. Frankly, I'm not so sure that you should want the pain to end. Don't misunderstand me. None of us enjoys pain. We all wish that we would just wake up some morning, only to discover to our hearts' delight that all of our emotional scars have suddenly vanished into thin air. Unfortunately, such wishful thinking is not realistic.

Pain is a very valuable commodity. Without it, you and I would become very cold, insensitive people. None of us wants to be a Vulcan. Our passion for helping people, our words of encouragement, the urgency with which we communicate our message, and our ability to relate to hurting people all flow out of the pain we carry.

Rather than asking God to remove your pain, pray for 2 Corinthians 1:3-4 to become a living reality in your life: "Praise be to the God and Father of our Lord Jesus Christ, the Father of compassion and the God of all comfort, who comforts us in all our troubles, *so that we can comfort those in any trouble with the comfort we ourselves have received from God*" (emphasis mine).

**Question:** "How can I be expected to trust this person after everything that he's done to me?"

**Answer:** As you read through the definitions of

forgiveness listed in chapter three, did you notice that I did not include the word "trust"? Trust and forgiveness are not synonymous. They do not overlap.

Forgiveness allows us to view the positive side of painful situations from God's perspective, and motivates us to move into the offender's life as a servant. But forgiveness does not demand that we trust the person.

Trust must be earned. If someone has violated our ability to trust him, then forgiveness would demand that we give the person ample opportunities to earn back our trust. Bitterness will close our hearts to the individual, making any restoration of the relationship impossible.


**Question:** "You mentioned that if I do not forgive, I will eventually become just like the person I hate. I have already begun to see similarities between me and the one who hurt me. Is there any hope? Can this process be reversed?"

**Answer:** I have good news for you. The process will begin to reverse itself the moment you begin to forgive.

Do you remember our discussion in chapter 2 concerning Proverbs 23:7? Negative thought patterns result in negative behavior. But the reverse is also true. Forgiveness will produce changes in your thinking concerning the person you formerly hated. Thus, your behavior will begin to change. Romans 12:2 summarizes our hope: "Be transformed by the renewing of your mind."

One word of warning: this transforming process takes time. Your behavior patterns probably took years to develop. Realistically, you cannot expect to reverse them overnight.

**Question:** "Do you still treat your children in the same way your dad treated you?"

**Answer:** I would give anything to be able to say, "No, never." But I cannot. On occasion I still find myself responding to those closest to me in the same way my dad responded to my mother, sisters, and me. I feel sometimes as though I am having a flashback. The words, "Like father, like son," can have a negative as well as a positive connotation.

When I do fail, I find God's declaration very reassuring: "My power is made perfect in weakness" (2 Corinthians 12:9). God's power in my life can be seen by my family in three ways: (1) My wife and children can see my genuinely broken heart as I stop and ask for their forgiveness. (2) They are reminded of the horrifying consequences of bitterness as they see them vividly lived out in my life. And (3) they can measure my spiritual growth as they see the frequency of my failure diminish over time.

**Question:** "What if I don't feel loving to the person?"

**Answer:** Forgiveness does not demand that you feel anything toward the person. The kind of love commanded in the Bible is volitional, not emotional. When God commanded us to "love one another" (1 John 4:7), He did not intend for us to break into euphoric goose-bumps every time a person's name flashes across our minds.

The Apostle John defined for us exactly what kind of love God commanded. He wrote, "Dear friends, since God so loved us, we also ought to love one another" (1 John 4:11). How did He love us? "He sent His one and only Son into the world that we might live through Him" (verse 9). Do you get the point? God demonstrated His love toward us by sacrificially meeting our deepest need. We, then, are commanded to sacrificially meet each other's needs.

Does this sound familiar? It should. We find ourselves right back to Romans 12:19 and 20: "Do not take revenge, my friends. On the contrary: 'If your enemy is hungry, feed him; if he is thirsty, give him something to drink.' " The passage says nothing about feelings. Do what is right regardless of your feelings.

**Question:** "How can I begin to restore a broken relationship if I don't even know where the person lives? He may be out of the state, or out of the country for that matter."

**Answer:** You can choose to forgive someone regardless of the geography involved. Don't allow your separation to stop you from taking the steps outlined in chapter 4.

If you would like to heal the relationship, I would encourage you to do the following. (1) Reread Matthew 5:23-24. Does this person have something against you? (2) If so, then think through the general categories of the offenses as I did in chapter 6. If you did become reunited with this person, how would you ask his forgiveness? Rehearse your words to him in your own mind. (3) I believe that one of the most fundamental dynamics of the Christian life can be found in the little two-word phrase mentioned in Daniel 1:8: "Daniel resolved." You need to make a resolution. Promise God that if He chooses to reunite you with this person, you will take the proper steps in restoring the relationship.

**Question:** "What should I do if I forgive someone, but he refuses to forgive me?"

**Answer:** In this situation, you have only one option: wait. God has not made you responsible for the other person's responses, only for your own. Remember the words of Romans 12:18: "If it is possible, as far as it depends on you, live at peace with everyone."

I can guarantee that difficult times will invade the other person's life, just as they have yours and mine. While you are waiting, make certain that you leave the door open so that he knows you will always be there when he needs you. View his trials as potential opportunities to demonstrate unconditional, sacrificial love.

**Question:** "You mentioned that at your dad's funeral, you felt thankful that your relationship was healed before it was too late. In my situation, the person died before I made things right. For me, it is already too late. Now what can I do?"

**Answer:** In actuality, it's not too late. It's not too late for you to forgive him. It's not too late for you to visualize the positive benefits that have come to your life because of his offenses. It's not too late for you to pass on to others what you have learned. It's not too late for God to transform your weaknesses into manifestations of His power. It's not too late for you to begin to reverse the process of becoming just like him. And it's not too late for you to become a servant to other people who might have been affected by him as you were.

**Question:** "What should I do if I wish to make things right with my dad, but my mom doesn't want me to contact him?"

**Answer:** Honor the wishes of your mother and pray that God will change her heart. You will find the governing principle in Proverbs 21:1: "The king's heart [and your mother's heart] is in the hand of the LORD; He directs it like a watercourse wherever He pleases."

I do not mean by this that I condone your mother's decision. But I do understand the emotions behind her concern. Apparently, your father hurt her quite deeply. Allowing you to reestablish a relationship with him now would only stir up some very painful memories. She needs time to deal with her own bitterness, and you need to give her that time.

I would, therefore, encourage you to do the following: (1) Reaffirm to your mother that you will not do anything against her will. (2) Determine the steps you will take in approaching your father if and when she gives you the green light. (3) Use your mother's protest as a clue to some needs in her life that you might be able to meet. (4) Ask God to use your mom to confirm for you the proper time in making contact with your dad.

**Question:** "I have taken all of the steps that you mentioned and still do not feel any different. Is something wrong?"

**Answer:** In relation to bitterness, I am asked about feelings more than any other single subject.

Again, our feelings are secondary. They need time to heal.

Study again the commands of Scripture. You will notice that they are nowhere tied to our emotions. The Bible does not say "If you feel like it, children, obey your parents." Or, "If you feel like it, fathers, do not exasperate your children." The Bible never conditions our obedience upon our emotions. Nor does the Bible guarantee that we will feel a certain way as a result of our obedience.

Our emotions can change with the wind and frankly cannot always be trusted. For this reason, Jeremiah wrote: "The heart is deceitful above all things and beyond cure. Who can understand it?" (Jeremiah 17:9) While we cannot understand our hearts, we can understand the clear commands of the Bible, and we can choose to do what we know is right, whether we feel like it or not.

**Question:** "I have been bitter toward someone for a long time. Now that I have forgiven her, is it enough to ask God to forgive me for my attitude of resentment? Do I have to ask the person to forgive me too? Should I confess my bitterness to my parents, my pastor, or the whole church?"

**Answer:** You need only to ask the forgiveness of those whom you have offended. If your parents or pastor are not involved, you do not need to tell them. If the person has no idea that you have harbored any bitterness, you do not need to tell her.

On occasion, someone has come up to me and said, "You know, Dewey, for years I have deeply resented you. I now know that I have been wrong. Would you forgive me for hating you so much?" To be honest with you, I would rather have never known!

Most of the time, however, people can pick up our hatred for them loud and clear. Therefore, under most circumstances, you will need to go to the person in the same manner in which I approached my dad.

**Question:** "You talk so openly about your painful experiences. I have been sexually abused. I don't want to tell anyone about it. Is it wrong for me to feel so ashamed?"

**Answer:** Certainly not. I feel ashamed about the way I responded to my father for all of those years.

Believe me, I am not proud of the fact that I used to pray that God would kill my dad. I do not delight in revealing to people the hatred that burned within me. I only share my story as a means of offering encouragement and counsel to others who are hurting.

You do not need to stand on a stage in front of throngs of people, telling them every sordid detail concerning your painful past. Rather, ask God to bring people into your life who have suffered in the same way as you. Simply let them know that you can relate because you have faced a similar situation. Tell them of your struggles and successes, always pointing them to the "God of all comfort," who seeks to comfort them as He has you and me.

**Question:** "I have forgiven others, but I can't seem to forgive myself. I feel so guilty because of some things that I have done. Is this normal? Can I do anything about it?"

**Answer:** The Bible refers to Satan as "the accuser of our brothers" (Revelation 12:10). He stands before

God, and He often stands before us, accusing us of our failures, making us feel dirty and cheap, when all the while God has declared us both cleansed and redeemed.

Romans 8:33-34 should end all guilt in the life of a believer. Paul wrote: "Who will bring any charge against those whom God has chosen? It is God who justifies [declares us 'Not guilty!']. Who is he that condemns? Christ Jesus, who died—more than that, who was raised to life—is at the right hand of God and is also interceding for us."

While guilt is never appropriate in the life of a believer, godly sorrow is. "Godly sorrow brings repentance" (2 Corinthians 7:10). When we rebel, we should feel a sense of sorrow because we have violated the One we love supremely. Godly sorrow should then cause us to have a change of mind about what we have done (repentance), and move us toward the confession our sins to God (1 John 1:9).

**Question:** "What did Jesus mean when He taught us to pray, 'Forgive us our debts, as we also have forgiven our debtors'? (Matthew 6:12) Does this mean that if I won't forgive someone, God won't forgive me? And if He won't forgive me, does that mean that I'll go to hell when I die?"

**Answer:** Matthew 6:12 has nothing to do with a person's salvation or eternal destiny. In the Bible, you will read about two kinds of forgiveness:

(1) Judicial forgiveness. This legal term refers to God, as the judge of the universe, declaring you "Not guilty!" the moment you received Jesus Christ as your Savior. This one-time declaration applies to your life as a whole, encompassing every sin (past,

present, and future), and secures your salvation forever.

(2) Relational forgiveness. Jesus had this in view when He gave the "Lord's Prayer" in Matthew 6. While your relationship with God is secure, areas of rebellion can effectively place a barrier between you and Him (Psalm 66:18), temporarily putting a strain on the relationship.

An unwillingness to forgive certainly qualifies as one type of rebellion. Listen to the words of the Apostle John: "If anyone says, 'I love God,' yet hates his brother, he is a liar. For anyone who does not love his brother, whom he has seen, cannot love God, whom he has not seen" (1 John 4:19-20). Your willingness to forgive will immediately shatter the barrier and your intimacy with God will be restored.

**Question:** "I honestly tried to think of some positive benefits that have resulted because of what I went through, but I can't think of any. Now what do I do?"

**Answer:** The final chapter has not yet been written in your life. The passage of time may reveal any or all of God's purposes in allowing your suffering to take place.

Quite honestly, I don't think that Job in the Bible would have been able to come up with any "positive benefits" either. He did not know about the behind-the-scenes confrontation between God and Satan. He could not possibly have anticipated the way in which he has become the symbol for "faithfulness in the midst of calamity" for all generations. One of life's greatest mysteries is this: "How in the world did Job handle his suffering so triumphantly when he didn't have the book of Job to help him through it?"

However, you do know that (1) God's power will be manifested through your weaknesses (2 Corinthians 12:7ff). (2) You will be much more effective in comforting others who are hurting (2 Corinthians 1:3ff). (3) God is at work in your life, transforming you into a person of character (Romans 5:3-5). (4) Your attraction to this world will decrease while your anticipation of the heavenly world to come will increase (Romans 8:22-25; Colossians 3:1-6). (5) God will draw close to you in the midst of your pain, since He promised to never leave or abandon you (Hebrews 13:5).

**Question:** "Like the girl you mentioned in chapter 4, I too was raped. The police caught the man, and I pressed charges. I have now forgiven him for what he did. Should I drop the charges? Am I wrong in testifying against him?"

**Answer:** No, do not drop the charges. You are not wrong in testifying against him. This man broke the law. God has ordained the government as His means of imposing upon lawbreakers a just punishment. Romans 13:1-5 clearly establishes this principle. Verse 4 gives a solemn warning to those considering a violent crime: "But if you do wrong, be afraid, for he [one in legal authority] does not bear the sword [an instrument of punishment] for nothing."

You now have the opportunity to help protect other innocent victims from this individual by getting him off the streets. Your testimony in a court of law will tremendously aid the judicial process.

**Question:** "I read a verse somewhere in the Bible about the father's sins affecting his children and perhaps even his grandchildren. Like you, I hated my father. Does this mean that my children will automatically hate me? Am I doomed to being a lousy father?"

**Answer:** You are referring to Exodus 20:5. This verse illustrates the principle of "influence." Do you realize that our lifestyle choices may influence our children's choices, even to three or four generations?

I can remember my mother and grandmother visiting our home shortly after my son was born. Four generations of people were represented in one living room. I could clearly see the reality of Exodus 20:5. What my grandmother did could profoundly influence what my son does, either positively or negatively.

Here's the good news: you can break the chain at any link. If you forgive your father, you can underscore, through your own experience, the dangers of allowing a root of bitterness to grow. You can, by example, teach your children how to love an unlovely person. You will be able to pass on to your children the rich heritage of learning how to "overcome evil with good" (Romans 12:21), with all of its attendant blessings.

**Question:** "Why do I become bitter toward someone I love? Is it because of a communication gap or is there more to it?"

**Answer:** The answer to your question hinges on the deadly word, "expectations." We basically become bitter toward people because they violate our expectations. They fail to respond to us in the manner we desire. In a word, they disappoint us.

I hope that my next statement does not sound pessimistic, but realistic. The longer I live, the more I expect people to live up to their depravity. Even so-called godly people.

Jesus said of His disciples, "The spirit is willing, but the body [flesh] is weak" (Mark 14:38). Paul said of himself in Romans 7:18: "I know that nothing good lives in me, that is, in my sinful nature ['flesh,' marginal reference]."

I can relate. When I became a Christian, I did not lose my flesh, nor did I escape its influence. How many times do I find myself doing the exact opposite of what I desire because I am trapped in my body of flesh, like a butterfly in a cocoon? Do I dare place on others a set of expectations that I myself cannot meet?

Living my life with this perspective has resulted in two rather profound realities. (1) When people do violate me, I am not surprised and I therefore do not get bitter. (2) When people come through for me, I am delirious with excitement and I communicate a sincere, heartfelt gratitude for what they have done.

My encouragement to you is to get rid of all your expectations and train yourself to take life as it comes, enjoying the good and enduring the bad. While this may sound a bit fatalistic, it sure beats anger, frustration, and bitterness every time somebody lets me down.

**Question:** "Will I ever get over my bitterness completely, or will I have to learn how to cope with it forever?"

**Answer:** I believe that you can get over your bitterness completely, but it will take time. Paul commanded the church at Colossae: "But now you must rid yourselves of all such things as these: anger, rage, malice, slander, and filthy language from your lips. Bear with one another and forgive whatever grievances you may have against one another. Forgive as the Lord forgave you" (Colossians 3:8, 13). God intends for you and me to obey that command.

But once again, it will take time. If God sees in your heart the genuine desire to obey these verses, He will be pleased. We will displease Him if we choose to resist His grace, and willingly allow a root of bitterness to grow up, defiling many (Hebrews 12:15).

## In the Trenches:
## Waging Your Own War from Within

1. Did any of the questions discussed in this chapter parallel any of your own? If so, what new insights did you gain from the answers?

2. What specific steps of action will you now take in light of this new information?

3. Do you have any questions that have not been answered? If so, use them as a motivation to study the Bible for yourself as you endeavor to find the answers. I would suggest the following passages as a starting point: Genesis 37–50 (the story of Joseph — look for any similarities between his situation and yours); Matthew 18:21-35; Romans 8:18-30; 12:9-21; Ephesians 4:17-32; and Colossians 3:1-17.

4. Can you think of anyone else who might benefit from this book? Why not give him a copy as an expression of your friendship and support? Share with him some of the specific ways in which this book has been of benefit to you.

5. I began this book by hinting at my foundational premise: "I write as one who has thoroughly studied the subject of bitterness from a biblical perspective." Now, I shall state my premise outright: The Bible is sufficient to meet every need of every heart.

I agree with Paul, who said, "All Scripture is God-breathed and is useful for teaching, rebuking, correcting and training in righteousness, so that the man of God may be thoroughly equipped for every good work" (2 Timothy 3:16-17).

I agree with Peter, who said, "His divine power has given us everything we need for life and godliness through our knowledge of Him" (2 Peter 1:3).

I agree with John, who recorded these words of Jesus' prayer, "Your Word is truth" (John 17:17).

I agree with David, who admonished us to never "walk in the counsel of the wicked," but rather to delight in and meditate on "the Law of the LORD." Then, we will be "like a tree planted by streams of water, which yields its fruit in season and whose leaf does not wither. Whatever he does prospers" (Psalm 1:1-3).

I agree with Joshua, who wrote, "Do not let this Book of the Law depart from your mouth; meditate on it day and night, so that you may be careful to do everything written in it. Then you will be prosperous and successful" (Joshua 1:8).

I agree with Jesus, who said, "I tell you the truth, until heaven and earth disappear, not the smallest letter, not the least stroke of a pen, will by any means disappear from the Law until everything is accomplished" (Matthew 5:18).

The Bible is sufficient! You need to turn to no other source than the Word of God. As you have discovered in its pages the answers concerning your "battle over bitterness," so continue to look to Scripture for the guidance you need in reference to every area of your life.

# Epilogue

*Therefore, if anyone is in Christ, he is a new creation; the old has gone, the new has come! (2 Corinthians 5:17)*

*V*ictory circle! Has there ever been a Christian camp that didn't end with a victory circle? Six hundred high school students jammed themselves, like sardines into a can, onto the benches surrounding the crackling fire. The eerie red glow of smoldering embers barely illuminated their faces.

With his guitar slung over his shoulder, a camp counselor led everyone in some choruses. Another took center stage and gave the instructions.

"We've had a great week together. God has done some unbelievable things. Many of you will be going home tomorrow as changed individuals. We want to hear about it. We are not here to praise your counsellor, or the speakers, or a friend. We want to direct our praises to God."

One by one the students stood and recounted story after story. A 16-year-old teen admitted that he brought drug paraphernalia from home. On Wednesday, he told us, he flushed his supply down the toilet. A 14-year-old broke down and wept as she vowed to stop rebelling against her parents. Several students declared that they had received Christ as their Savior. For an hour and a half, a holy hush permeated the scene as dozens of people asked for prayer and encouragement.

High above the silhouettes of the campers, screened from their view by the elongated shadows of the nearby evergreens, I sat alone, listening and thinking. I reviewed the week, replaying the many interviews, discussions, and counseling sessions that had taken place. I had met many students and unfortunately most of them would gradually fade into my memory as a sea of nameless faces. A very few, however, for one reason or another, would never be forgotten.

Julie fits into this latter category. I could not get over the unnerving impact of her words. Over and over again I could hear her scream, "Jesus, go to hell."

I had not seen Julie since our conversation at the beginning of the week. I had no idea how she was doing. Some counselors half-expected her to slice her wrists again, if she didn't hitchhike home first. From my veiled vantage point, I tried in vain to pick her out of the crowd seated below me but the light was too dim. I wondered if she was even there.

I glanced at my watch. Eleven-thirty! Time seemed to move so quickly. Joe took his place on the platform and announced, "Before we move into our communion service, does any one else have anything they would like to say?"

For the first time that evening, Julie's cries became audible. Directly above and behind Joe, a group of bodies began rumbling across the back bench. Two of Julie's friends helped her to her feet. She brushed back her tears, and began to speak. Nobody moved.

"I hated this place when I got here," Julie recalled. "I thought to myself. 'You're all a bunch of flaky hypocrites.' I only went to the meetings because my counselor forced me. I sat in the back and refused to listen.

"Dewey really ticked me off. Why did he have to say all that stuff about his father the other night? I didn't want to think about my family. I came here to get away. But he just kept talking. I tried to block his words from affecting me. As he spoke, I thought about my parents and how much I hated them.

"I tried to run away during his speech, but my counselor found me. She brought me back to the chapel, and we waited while Dewey talked to some of you. Then he met with me.

"You should have seen the look on his face," Julie chuckled. "I guess I really shocked him. Some of you were there and looked pretty funny, too. He told me that I could tell Jesus anything I wanted. So I did. I told Him where I thought He could go. 'Go to hell,' that's what I said. And I meant it.

"But all week long, I haven't been able to forget what Dewey said to me after that. My parents would have slapped me with the back of their hand. They would have cussed at me and kicked me out of the house. But he didn't do anything like that. None of you did. My counselor put her arm around me and

**125**

hugged me. No one ever hugs me. And Dewey calmly looked at me, and told me something that has changed my life."

I shivered in the shadows as the mountain air began to turn crisp and cool. All eyes remained glued to Julie. The small wisps of smoke rising from the burned-out logs gave mute testimony to the stillness of the night air, almost as if even nature held its breath in anticipation of what she would say next.

"When I told Jesus to go to hell, Dewey just looked at me and said, 'Julie, He already did. He answered that prayer 2,000 years ago.' "

Julie broke down. She could not continue. Her friends and counselor tried to comfort her.

Finally, she regained her composure, and stood up one last time. Through her tears, she stammered, "I never thought that anyone loved me. Now I know that Jesus does. He loved me enough to suffer my punishment of hell in my place. And I just want you to know that I love Jesus, and I love all of you. I'm going to go home tomorrow and tell my parents that I now love them."

I leaned back against a tree, knowing I had just witnessed a modern-day miracle. Only God could have changed Julie's heart. With His help, she won her battle over bitterness.

How about you? What about your battle? Are you winning or losing it? It is my hope that through the principles outlined in this book, you will experience the ultimate victory of being able to pluck up those wretched weeds of bitterness and anger by their ravishing roots, never to cultivate them again. May God be ever near to you as you seek His strength in doing so.

For we do not have a High Priest [Jesus] who is unable to sympathize with our weaknesses, but we have One who has been tempted in every way, just as we are—yet was without sin. Let us then approach the throne of grace with confidence, so that we may receive mercy and find grace to help us in our time of need (Hebrews 4:15-16).

# NOTES

## Chapter 2

1. *The Sunset Western Garden Book* (Menlo Park, Calif: Sunset Books, 1988), 56.

2. Jay Carty, *Counterattack* (Portland: Multnomah Press, 1988), 73.

3. S.I. McMillen, *None of These Diseases* (Old Tappan, N.J.: Fleming H. Revell, 1977), 63, 69.

4. Paul D. Meier, Frank B. Minirth, and Frank B. Wickern, *Introduction to Psychology and Counseling* (Grand Rapids: Baker Book House, 1982), 261.

5. McMillen, *None of These Diseases*, 72.

6. Meier, *Introduction to Psychology and Counseling*, 261.

7. Ibid.

8. Ibid., 262.

9. *The Life Application Book* (Wheaton, Ill.: Tyndale House, 1988), 856.

10. Ibid, 1337.

11. Carty, *Counterattack,* 72–73.

12. "Daily News L.A. Weekend Magazine," 27 October, 1989, 63.

## Chapter 3

1. *Funk and Wagnalls New Encyclopedia,* vol. 9, 276.

## Chapter 5

1. *The Life Application Bible,* 1723.

2. Ibid.